THE TWENTIETH CENTURY HOUSE IN BRITAIN

THE TWENTIETH
CENTURY HOUSE
IN BRITAIN

FROM THE ARCHIVES OF COUNTRY LIFE

ALAN POWERS

AURUM PRESS

In memory of John Cornforth

First published in Great Britain 2004 by Aurum Press Limited
25 Bedford Avenue, London WC1B 3AT

Text copyright © 2004 by Alan Powers
Photographs © *Country Life* Picture Library

ISBN 1 84513 012 X
10 9 8 7 6 5 4 3 2 1
2008 2007 2006 2005 2004

Design by James Campus
Originated by Colorlito-CST Srl, Milan
Printed and bound in Singapore by CS Graphics

Half-title page: *Tile mosaic floor at Yaffle Hill, Dorset, depicting the house.*
Frontispiece: *The foot of the stairs at The Homewood, Surrey, by Patrick Gwynne.*
Front endpaper: *Roman grandeur by Philip Tilden at Port Lympne, Kent.*
Rear endpaper: *A Modernist roof terrace by William Lescaze at High Cross House, Devon.*

THE COUNTRY LIFE PICTURE LIBRARY

The *Country Life* Picture Library holds a complete set of prints made from its negatives, and a card index to the subjects, usually recording the name of the photographer and the date of the photographs catalogued, together with a separate index of photographers. It also holds a complete set of *Country Life* and various forms of published indices to the magazine. The Library may be visited by appointment, and prints of any negatives it holds can be supplied by post.

For further information, please contact the Librarian, Camilla Costello, at *Country Life*, King's Reach Tower, Stamford Street, London SE1 9LS (*Tel:* 020 7261 6337).

ACKNOWLEDGEMENTS

I am grateful to Michael Hall for commissioning me to write this book and giving valuable advice in the early stages, and to Jeremy Musson who took over Michael's role. Special thanks are due to Camilla Costello and her colleagues in the *Country Life* Picture Library for making research there such a pleasure. I am grateful to James Campus for his sympathy with the material as the book's designer, and to Clare Howell for her patience and understanding as its editor.

Without the opportunities I have had during the past fifteen years to write regular articles for *Country Life* on houses of the twentieth century, I should not have been in a position to write this book. I am grateful to the successive architectural editors, Clive Aslet, Giles Worsley, Michael Hall and Jeremy Musson, for their encouragement. The photographers down the years have contributed to making the houses look their best. I would like to mention in particular June Buck and Clive Boursnell, who have taken the pictures for many of my articles. The owners of the houses that I have visited in the course of research have also contributed their knowledge, enthusiasm and hospitality. My family have, as always, provided support as well as necessary diversion from the task.

LIST OF ARTICLES

This is a list of *Country Life* articles for which the photographs reproduced in this book were taken. The photographer's name is given (in brackets) if known.

Port Lympne, Kent: 19 and 26 May 1923 (A. E. Henson); 4 February 1933.
Bron-y-Dê, Surrey: 4 November 1922.
Coleton Fishacre, Devon: 31 May 1930 (A. E. Henson).
Cour, Argyllshire: 13 August 1992 (June Buck).
Hammels, Oxfordshire: 10 and 17 March 1923 (Sleigh).
Oare House, Wiltshire: 10 March 1928 (Westley).
No. 42 Cheyne Walk, London: 14 and 21 January 1933 (A. E. Henson).
Woodfalls, Hampshire: 23 March 1929 (Newbery); 4 October 1930.
Shepherd's Hill, Sussex: 9 October 1975 (Jonathan Gibson).
Gayfere House, London: 13 February 1932 (A. E. Henson).

High and Over, Buckinghamshire: 19 September 1931 (Newbery).
High Cross House, Devon: 11 February 1933 (A. E. Henson); 3 August 1995 (June Buck).
Yaffle Hill, Dorset: 8 July 1933 (A. E. Henson).
Ashcombe Tower, Devon: 13 February 1937; 12 December 1996 (June Buck).
Eltham Palace, London: 15, 22 and 29 May 1937 (A. E. Henson); 9 November 1995 (June Buck).
Templewood, Norfolk: 4 February 1939 (Thompson).
Charters, Berkshire: 24 November and 1 and 8 December 1944 (Westley).
Gribloch, Stirlingshire: 12 and 19 January 1951 (Westley); 12 February 1998 (June Buck).
Birchens Spring, Buckinghamshire: 29 January and 5 February 1938 (A. E. Henson); 9 January 1997 (June Buck).
Chapel Point, Cornwall: 19 and 26 October 1945 (Westley).
Ridgemead, Surrey: 10 and 17 February 1940 (Thompson and A. E. Henson).
Buttersteep House, Berkshire: 2 January 1942.
The Homewood, Surrey: 22 July 1993 (Mark Fiennes).
No. 2 Willow Road, London: 12 September 1991 (Michael Boys).
Monkton House, Sussex: 12 September 1985 (Jonathan Gibson).
Bentley Wood, Sussex: 26 October and 2 November 1940 (Thompson); 19 April 2001 (Thompson).
The Studio, Highgate, London: 26 March 1998 (June Buck).
Great House, Essex: 10 November 1950 (Turnley).
No. 20 Blackheath Park, London: 31 July 1958 (Alex Starkey); 4 May 2000 (June Buck).
No. 19 North End, London: 12 November 1959 (Alex Starkey).
Upper Wolves Copse, Sussex: 4 December 1958 (Alex Starkey).
No. 6 Bacon's Lane, London: 25 January 2001 (Julian Nieman).
Toys Hill, Kent: 7 August 1958 (Alex Starkey).
The Walled Garden, Berkshire: 11 August 1960 (Scarbro).
Farnley Hey, Yorkshire: 7 January 1993 (June Buck).
High Sunderland, Borders: 15 September 1960.
No. 16 Kevock Road, Lasswade, Midlothian: 11 February 1960.
Serenity, Surrey: 14 September 1958.
The Studio, Hemingford Grey, Huntingdonshire: 12 September 2002 (June Buck).
Weston Patrick House, Hampshire: 13 October 1960.
Provost's Lodgings, Queen's College, Oxford: 7 July 1960.
St Vedast Rectory, London: 2 June 1960.
Meols Hall, Lancashire: 25 January and 1 and 8 February 1973 (Alex Starkey).
No. 3 Church Walk, Aldeburgh, Suffolk: 2 October 1997 (June Buck).
Cray Clearing, Oxfordshire: 6 April 1967 (Alex Starkey).
The Spender Studio, Maldon, Essex: 23 September 1999 (June Buck).
Heathbrow, London: 9 May 1963 (Alex Starkey).
Pentice Walk, Surrey: 19 September 1963 (Jonathan Gibson).
Arundel Park, Sussex: 20 June 1996 (June Buck).
Lushill House, Wiltshire: 26 October 1989 (Jonathan Gibson).
Sunderlandwick, Yorkshire: 1, 18 and 25 October 1984 (Alex Starkey).
Bentley Farm, Sussex: 13 and 20 September 1984 (Jonathan Gibson).
Wivenhoe New Park, Essex: 22 July 1965 (Jonathan Gibson).
King's Walden Bury, Hertfordshire: 27 September and 4 October 1973 (Alex Starkey).
Pillwood, Cornwall: 7 August 2003 (Clive Boursnell).
Gorsfach, Gwynedd: 15 November 2001 (Alex Ramsay).
Castell Gryn, Clwyd: 29 September 1991 (Mark Fiennes).
Barley Splatt, Cornwall: 30 May 1985 (Mark Fiennes).
The New House, Sussex: 17 July 1986 (Mark Fiennes).
Merks Hall, Essex: 7 July 1988 (Tim Imrie-Tait).
Henbury Hall, Cheshire: 28 February 2002 (Tim Imrie-Tait).
Ashfold House, Sussex: 7 November 1991 (June Buck).
Baggy House, Devon: 26 September 1996 (Clive Boursnell).
The New House, Surrey: 3 September 1998 (June Buck).
The Old Rectory, Sussex: 3 September 1998 (June Buck).
Dunesslin, Dumfriesshire: 13 July 2000 (Paul Barker).
Westlake Brake, Devon: 30 April 1998 (Clive Boursnell).
Nos. 1A and 1B Kingdon Avenue, Prickwillow, Cambridgeshire: 13 November 2003 (June Buck).
The Lawns, London: 31 January 2002 (Julian Nieman).

Articles on The Anderton House, No. 62 Camden Mews, No. 3 Clarkson Road, and Creek Vean will be published in *Country Life* during 2004–05.

CONTENTS

*

THIS book surveys new houses from an eighty-year period – 1920 to 2000 – using photographs from the *Country Life* Picture Library. Since its foundation in 1897, the magazine has consistently published a superbly illustrated weekly article on country houses, and it soon developed a strong interest in contemporary domestic architecture that has continued to this day, in conjunction with its definitive surveys of historic homes.

The story being told here is, then, partly a story about actual houses and the people who built them, and partly a story about a magazine and its reasons for selecting what was photographed and published – not necessarily the same thing, since a large number of the new houses featured were illustrated with photographs provided by the architects, and therefore not retained in the library. Nonetheless, there is no visual resource for the study of this subject that is remotely comparable to *Country Life*, and the selection in this book represents only what we have considered to be the best.

Inevitably, the building of new houses raises all sorts of issues, such as the evolution of house plans in relation to social changes: fewer servants, the rise in central heating, the type of people who commissioned the houses, and the type of architects they chose. In addition, there are aspects of the houses closely tied to their architecture, such as interior decoration, garden design and landscape. These topics are touched on in the book, but in this introduction I want to focus on the differences in architectural styles that are so evident in the houses, from the beginning to the end of this period.

The writing in *Country Life* reveals a complex story about the reception of modern architecture in Britain that has not been fully investigated before.[1] Journals specialising in architecture and design often adopt an attitude that effectively preselects their material, but *Country Life*, as readers unfamiliar with the magazine may be surprised to discover, has usually been pluralist and inclusive in its architectural tastes. It faced the world in this tolerant spirit in 1920, and finished the century in much the same mood. Before the concept of chaos theory – the recognition of patterns in seemingly random events – was formulated, *Country Life* had unwittingly developed its own chaotic historiography.

In 1920, revival styles were dominant in all areas of British design. Modernism was more recognisable as a concept in painting and sculpture than in architecture, and almost ten years passed before Modernist architecture in Europe penetrated Britain. Yet the need to find 'a style of our own time' was already several generations old and had long worried British architects as much as foreign ones. Furthermore, not all aspects of the 'New Architecture' were entirely new or alien. Although the literal representation of historic styles typical of the 1920s in Britain was contrary to its principles, other aspects, such as open planning, large windows and contact with the outdoors, were derived from late-Victorian Arts and Crafts houses in Britain that reflected past styles and rejected industrial civilisation.

Conversely, Modernism is full of hidden references to traditional and regional architecture, while traditional-looking houses usually incorpo-rated the latest technology, as in Neo-Tudor mansions with their electric lights and luxurious bathrooms. Neo-Georgian plan layouts responded to changing patterns of life almost as much as modern ones. The message given by the formal language of the architecture is, therefore, often a deceptive one if it is interpreted as a simple indication of looking forwards or looking backwards.

While it may seem obvious in retrospect that the split between Modernism and its opposite was not a clean break, it seldom seemed that way to architects. Starting in 1836 with A. W. N. Pugin's *Contrasts*, and continuing with John Ruskin's *Seven Lamps of Architecture* in 1849, the English architectural mind absorbed the idea that one's choice of architectural style indicated a belief system, good or bad. In the view of Pugin and Ruskin, Renaissance Classicism was bad. The Modernists of the 1930s took the same attitude, although their alternative was not Gothic, but a supposedly new style.

If Modernism between the wars had flourished as yet one more style in the range of choices, as it did for Oliver Hill and some other inter-war architects, then our story would be different, but from the beginning it was an issue on which people felt obliged to take sides, and so it remains today. Ironically, it was the concept of architectural style, from which modern architects claimed to be escaping, that remained a dominating concern for them; they became, as the architect H. S. Goodhart-Rendel put it in the 1930s, 'inconscient slaves of their own styleless stylism'.[2]

It is often assumed that the 'battle of the styles' between the wars can be represented as an uphill struggle for Modernism, but one in which steady progress was made. The evidence is more complex, however,

GLEDSTONE HALL, YORKSHIRE (1922–26) Above: *Gledstone epitomises the last phase of Classical design by Sir Edwin Lutyens, the greatest country-house architect of his generation.*

YAFFLE HILL, DORSET (1930) Left: *The design by Sir Edward Maufe made a compromise between tradition and Modernism typical of its period. The Mediterranean look was widely copied.*

and therefore more interesting. Taking *Country Life* as the sample for evidence, the first encounter with home-grown Modernism was the white-painted, flat-roofed houses with strongly horizontal windows at Silver End, Essex, by Thomas Tait (1882–1954), published in 1928. The description by Randal Phillips explained that similar oddities had been appearing for some while on the Continent, but asserted the presence of tradition and precedent concealed beneath the appearance of novelty. While he admitted that 'Mr Tait's [houses] do bear the stamp of a new thing', Phillips correctly claimed that 'there have been plenty of flat roofs in England', for example in the work of the Manchester architect Edgar Wood.[3]

Phillips made what would become a standard defence of Modernism: that it was logical and practical, and 'in the spirit of our own day', in the same way that car design was a direct solution of practical problems.[4] There was support for an open-minded attitude towards ending Britain's obsession with the past, by way of an architecture that might make people better able to see the deplorable reality of their condition and take steps to improve it. The contrast between Arthur Rackham's standard illustration of a castle representing 'modern domestic architecture' at the top of the magazine's pages, and examples such as Silver End, was evidence of the divided culture. As a *Country*

Life editorial of 1933 proposed, 'at least we can bring rational design into our homes, and so make a beginning in our task of re-shaping the world'.[5]

Christopher Hussey (1899–1970), who joined *Country Life* as an architectural writer in 1920, belonged in the later 1920s to a small discussion group centred on Le Corbusier's *Vers une architecture* (1923), the most widely read Modernist manifesto. His own articles charted with approval the emergence of a simpler style of furniture out of the background of the Arts and Crafts movement. The English love of the past had become a rampant infection that needed to be restrained, if necessary by strong medicine, but two articles in 1930 by Noel Carrington reported on small Swedish houses, mostly built of timber, which demonstrated a less extreme kind of Modernism than Le Corbusier, and reflected national tradition without 'self-conscious traditionalism'.

HIGH AND OVER, BUCKINGHAMSHIRE (1929–31) Above: *Bernard Ashmole's study was designed by Amyas Connell with fitted furniture in a restrained style, including 'a dream of a desk for the literary'.*

SILVER END GARDEN VILLAGE, ESSEX (1927) Right: *How* Country Life *presented Thomas Tait's surprising white cubic houses built for managers and workers at the Crittall window factory.*

MODERN DOMESTIC ARCHITECTURE

SOME HOUSES AT SILVER END GARDEN VILLAGE, ESSEX,
DESIGNED BY MR. THOMAS S. TAIT.

WHEN Inigo Jones came home from Italy in the seventeenth century, he brought the Renaissance in his pocket, but the conditions then existing were such that the dissemination of classical design was bound to be a very slow process. To day it is quite otherwise. Easy facilities of travel and the abounding illustrations of the Press make everyone almost immediately familiar with what is being done abroad. Nevertheless, the houses here shown have the special interest of a new thing. They belong to a type which, since the war, has been largely exploited in France, Germany, Holland, Denmark and Sweden, but, with the single exception of one at Northampton, these are the first houses of their kind to be erected in England. Mr. Thomas S. Tait (of Sir John Burnet and Partners) has evolved them, and at the outset it must be stated that he has done so not with the idea of producing anything that is freakish, but frankly as a logical and practical expression of design and building in the spirit of our own day. He has approached his problem in just the same way as a motor car designer, but supplemented by those æsthetic principles which form part of an architect's make-up.

ENTRANCE FRONT TO MANAGER'S HOUSE.

The most noticeable thing about these houses is that they have flat roofs, but, of course, there is nothing new in this. There have been plenty of flat roofs in England. Years ago Mr. Edgar Wood made some very successful essays in flat-roofed country houses, and many of those erected since the war on the Kennington estate of the Duchy of Cornwall (from designs by Messrs. Adshead and Ramsey) are similarly roofed. At Braintree, too, not many miles away from these houses at Silver End, some flat-roofed concrete-block houses were erected in 1919 from a "unit" design devised by Mr. C. H. B. Quennell and Mr. W. F.

Crittall. So, as I say, there is nothing new in the flat roof. Nevertheless, these houses of Mr. Tait's do bear the stamp of a new thing. The whole treatment of the elevations has as much to do with it as the flat roofs.

This garden village at Silver End, half way between Braintree and Witham, is in course of development by a subsidiary undertaking of The Crittall Manufacturing Company, whose works for the manufacture of standardised metal windows are at Braintree, Witham and Maldon. The centre of its being is a factory employing over three hundred men, the majority of

ANOTHER MANAGER'S HOUSE, AND DETAIL OF ENTRANCE FRONT.

There was a brief period during which highly theatrical interiors with mirror glass, like those at Finella, Cambridge, by Raymond McGrath, published in 1930, or Gayfere House in London by Oliver Hill, were seen as representative of Modernism. Some of the houses published in *Country Life*, such as Edward Maufe's Yaffle Hill or Brian O'Rorke's Ashcombe Tower, have special interest today because they combine a relatively traditional exterior with modern interiors that were decorative in their Modernism. We now call these interiors Art Deco, a conveniently open-ended term that could cover much of what the magazine published between the wars that was neither pure modern nor pure period. By the middle of the 1930s, the style that Osbert Lancaster called 'Vogue Regency' emerged as a replacement for Art Deco.

Men of taste like Hussey, schooled on the best work of the past, preferred their Modernism to display decorum and restraint. Amyas Connell's High and Over, built for a professor of Classical archaeology and published in 1931, was presented as a return to the essential spirit of Ancient Greece; almost before Modernism had begun, it was already being explained as an aspect of the past. While Hussey's text acknowledges that some special pleading is necessary for such an outspoken design, he gave modern architecture the benefit of the doubt because it was preferable to the alternatives, such as 'the most bogus types of "engagement ring" domiciles, which are true neither to the standards of good architecture nor to the spirit of the age'.[6]

The honeymoon phase of *Country Life*'s relationship with Modernism culminated in the Exhibition of British Industrial Art in Relation to the Home, held in the summer of 1933 at the Dorland Hall in Regent Street. Hussey chaired the organising committee, the chief designer and selector was Oliver Hill, and *Country Life* provided financial backing. The exhibition was an extraordinary and unprecedented event that established the character of mainstream British Modernism as moderate but not dull, owing to Hill's sense of fun and good eye for colour and form.

In his book *Modernismus* (1934), the elderly architect Reginald Blomfield had warned his readers: 'The New Architecture has become a "stunt" ... the most fatal of all obstacles to real and permanent progress.'[7] Modernism still tried to promote itself on the basis of scientific efficiency, but it soon became clear that in achieving an artistic impact, efficiency was often impaired. Only a few observers realised that the real qualities of the New Architecture lay in a different direction, as John Summerson explained in a *Country Life* supplement in February 1937, comparing a Neo-Georgian house on the Dartington Estate by Oswald Milne with a modern house, Shrub's Wood at Chalfont St Giles, by Mendelsohn and Chermayeff. He made the paradoxical claim that the modern house was romantic and exciting, and the traditional one practical but boring. 'The sweep of the Chalfont plan, its generous terrace and dramatic asymmetry, all have a tremendous psychological appeal,' Summerson wrote. 'Here is a "space consciousness" very like what the Elizabethans must have felt when they added long windowed galleries to their old halls, opening out their houses to the light and the newly-discovered pleasures of English landscape and Italian garden.'[8]

THE WOOD HOUSE, KENT (1936–37) Top: *Walter Gropius used timber to soften the impact of modern design.*

Above: *The entrance to the Exhibition of British Industrial Art in Relation to the Home (1933), designed by Oliver Hill, emphasised the simple beauty of everyday tools and implements.*

Writers outside the world of architecture cared less about a balanced approach, believing that if Regency or late-Georgian were the best styles, they should simply be imitated again. In a letter of 1934, Oliver Brooke complained of two new buildings in a Surrey village, one a sweet shop in 'shamtique' style, the other in 'the residential style that imitates a factory', and enquired 'why this country, which until the Regency built houses that were the admiration of foreign visitors, is now so barren in the department wherein it formerly excelled'.[9]

Evelyn Waugh's article 'A Call to the Orders', which appeared in the *Country Life* supplement of 26 February 1938, declared that for ten or fifteen years Britain had experienced 'villas like sewage farms, mansions like half-submerged Channel steamers' and similar architectural horrors, but that after a while 'the triumphs of the New Architecture began to assume the melancholy air of a deserted exhibition'.[10] All this, Waugh suggested, was an aberration, and that 'on our convalescence from the post-war Corbusier plague that has passed over us' architects and clients were turning again to Classical models, particularly late-Georgian examples.

He had a good point, for the architects of the early 1930s, fixated though they were on science and the vision of the future, tended to design as if the sun always shone and as if rainwater moved upwards rather than streaking down concrete walls and ponding on flat roofs. In particular, many 1930s Modernist houses were built of brick but covered in render to present a smooth surface. The more technically advanced the materials of the render, the more likely it was to let in water and crack in frost.

Many architects took care not to repeat these faults. Walter Gropius, seen by conservatives as one of the bogeymen of Modernism for his role in founding the Bauhaus school in 1919, built The Wood House at Shipbourne, Kent, in 1936, during his three-year exile in London, using

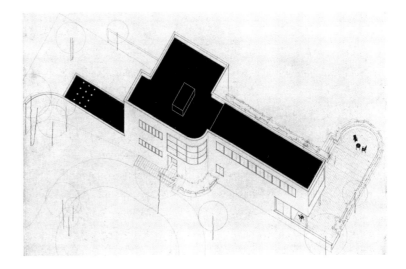

BAILIFFSCOURT, SUSSEX (1931) Above: *Lord Moyne's house was an instant antiquity.*

Top right: *In a 1937 article, John Summerson asked: 'Why search for anything new?', contrasting Oswald Milne's house on the Dartington Estate (above) with the romance of Modernism, exemplified in this design for Shrub's Wood, Buckinghamshire, by Mendelsohn and Chermayeff (below), to demonstrate the answer.*

timber, the same material chosen by Serge Chermayeff for Bentley Wood, designed the following year.

At The Studio in Highgate, London, Tayler and Green took care to learn from the mistakes of their predecessors by specifying a weak three-coat render for their walls, a revival of a traditional building technique for modern purposes. By 1947, Lionel Brett could write, 'the modern house which started life, as adolescents must, by fighting its environment, seemed, as the decade ended, to be coming to terms with it'.[11]

From these examples, one can see the beginnings of a possible 1940s style of Modernism beginning to emerge. As Arthur Oswald wrote in 1939, 'the new vigour which the modernist has brought to architecture will not be dissipated, at the same time his attitude of the rigid doctrinaire will have to be modified'.[12] Because of the Second World War, the development of 1940s Modernism was arrested, although the houses named above were often among those published as exemplars during and after the war, and their lessons were learnt to the extent that a flat-roofed white house in the 1950s seemed hopelessly out of date. Writing in 1940, John Summerson, so recently the advocate of Modernism as a revival of the romantic spirit, admitted that 'architectural design is still an affair of compromise'.[13]

What kind of buildings provided a valid case for an alternative to Modernism between the wars? They were broadly speaking Medieval,

GODMERSHAM PARK, KENT (1935) *This historic house, associated with Jane Austen, was re-Georgianised, as depicted amid immaculate lawns by Rex Whistler in 1938.*

Tudor or Classical. Many were literal in their attempt to recreate the past, reflecting the high value placed on older houses of a smaller size which were being restored for modern living throughout this period.

Bailiffscourt, near Bognor Regis in Sussex, built in 1930 by antique-dealer architect Amyas Phillips as a seaside retreat for Lord Moyne, the Guinness peer, is one example out of many houses that reused salvaged parts of old buildings; another was Hammels, near Oxford. Popular though these time-travelling houses might be, their progeny was the despised suburban villa, and they could not be advocated as a universal solution.

With its long and almost continuous history from the ancient world onwards, Classicism can be imagined without reference to specific moments in the past. Sir Edwin Lutyens, to take the style's most prominent twentieth-century exponent, valued the precision of Classicism, making some of his houses as complex as a Swiss watch, but this was for the sake of the game, rather than to make fake history. Setting standards of design or execution that were almost unattainable by others, Lutyens overshadowed all country-house architects in the inter-war period and even beyond. His work is deliberately under-represented in this book, because of the companion volume in this series by Gavin Stamp, *Edwin Lutyens Country Houses* (2001).

Lutyens' successors could pay tribute by imitation (and many did, whether they were his son Robert, pupils such as Oswald Milne, or admirers such as Oliver Hill). If Classicism was their passion, like Raymond Erith, they might consider Lutyens too Romantic and

Picturesque. Even Modernists could attribute their choice of style to the impossibility of beating Lutyens at his own game.

Seely and Paget's Templewood in Norfolk shows how a house might offend both Modernist and Classicist taste. It makes light of Classical rules despite using salvaged parts from eighteenth-century buildings. Paradoxically, its plan form is a more accurate re-creation of a Palladio villa than most English Palladian houses of the eighteenth century, while also offering a novel way to organise small rooms around a large one at the centre.

Other architects besides Erith were happy to respond to Waugh's call for a renewed appreciation of late-Georgian style. One of the grandest examples was Great Swifts in Cranbrook, Kent, designed by Geddes Hyslop for Major Victor Cazalet, and commended by Arthur Oswald for being 'restrained and sympathetic'. A similar coolness of character, owing little to Lutyens' theatricality, can be seen in remodellings of historic houses published in *Country Life*, such as Godmersham Park, Kent, altered for Robert Tritton by Walter Sarrel, and Castle Hill, Devon, rebuilt after a fire by Gerald Wellesley and Trenwith Wills.[14] One can almost recognise a 'George VI' style of tightly buttoned Neo-Georgian emerging from the pages of *Country Life* at this time.

The Regency style was also fashionable. Landhurst, Sussex, was completed in 1939 by a young architect, Louis Osman, but appeared in

Country Life only in 1949, when Arthur Oswald wrote that Landhurst offered 'the architect of today a firm foundation on which to build; a railhead at the end of the long line of classical tradition'.[15]

A house such as Kibes in Rotherfield Grays, Oxfordshire, designed by Florence Gibb and Margaret Low in 1938, sits as nearly as possible on an imagined line where late-Georgian and modern meet. Its balconied bow is a reminder of The White House at Shiplake, not far away, designed in 1900 by George Walton, a previous moment of encounter between late-Georgian and a Modernism still awaiting birth.

The New House in Crockham Hill, Kent, designed by Hugh Spencely for himself and also published in 1938, has a projecting cornice to tie together its brick walls, but otherwise moves, like Basil Spence's Gribloch, Stirlingshire, a step further towards Modernism.[16] As discussed in Chapter 2, the search for a credible middle position was often the theme used by Christopher Hussey to introduce his articles on new houses. Some of his swans, like Hamstone House, Surrey, by Forbes and Tate, now look more like geese, although others, such as the houses of John Campbell, were interesting because the designer's answer had been found in vernacular rather than Classical sources, suggesting a completely different way of seeing the history of architecture.[17]

The history of the relationship between tradition and Modernism between the wars has been explored here at some length, as this was a period when private house design was still an important indication of architectural trends on a broader scale, and *Country Life* offers one of the best sources of such information. Many things changed after the war, starting with the drastic reduction in the scale of any new houses being built. Given that stringency was unavoidable, this was not necessarily a disadvantage, and architects of all stylistic persuasions showed their skill in providing agreeable living spaces on a smaller scale. One of the crucial differences arising from the decline in

domestic service – and its associated culture of class distinction – was the potential to design a house 'in the round', without having one 'dead' side involving a tradesmen's entrance and kitchen window. The benefits can be seen in the pure geometry of houses such as No. 3 Clarkson Road, Cambridge. Dwellers in Classical houses were more likely to stick to old ways, but at Weston Patrick, Hampshire, and Sunderlandwick, Yorkshire, the service accommodation is placed in linked but architecturally distinct pavilions alongside the house.

If open planning was one of the supposed benefits of Modernism, then post-war conditions encouraged architects to go far beyond their tentative pre-war steps in this direction. Many of the houses published in *Country Life* overcame their small scale by demonstrating complex interior landscapes of linked rooms and changing levels, made physically possible by central heating.

The period from 1955 to 1970 was one of the most stimulating for domestic architecture in the history of Britain, and *Country Life* included a new house in almost every issue. New writers such as Mark Girouard did not share the hesitations Christopher Hussey had expressed about Modernism before the war, partly because Modernism itself had changed, regularly using timber and brick rather than concrete, and drawing inspiration from vernacular sources without interpreting them too literally.

The magazine continued to represent all the styles in evidence, however, and included a number of houses in which the pre-war 'middle way' was explored in a new manner. Millstones at Beaconsfield, Buckinghamshire, for example, designed by Roger Simmons in 1958, was published under the title 'Traditional or Flat Roofs', displaying its neo-vernacular tiled slopes with a confidence rarely seen since the 1920s.[18] Then there was the 'Contemporary Style' associated with the Festival of Britain, which filled to some extent the same in-between area of design as pre-war Art Deco, and was exemplified at Farnley Hey in Yorkshire; but, as with Art Deco, *Country Life* usually tried to see beyond fashion to establish new principles for house design with some form of historical foundation.

In the period of inflation and oil crisis around the early 1970s, the

GREAT SWIFTS, KENT (1938) Above: *A new house by Geddes Hyslop, displaying a Georgian style no longer under the spell of Lutyens.*

HAMSTONE HOUSE, SURREY (1938) Top right: *A design by Forbes and Tate, offering a new way of marrying Modernism and Georgian style.*

supply of good new houses became much more restricted. John Cornforth's text for King's Walden Bury, Hertfordshire, in 1973 marks a moment of change. This was no longer the guarded approval given by Mark Bence-Jones in 1965 to Raymond Erith's Wivenhoe New Park in Essex, but rather a call to arms against Modernism with a substantial Classical house to show the way. *Country Life* played a vital role during the 1970s in promoting conservation, not only of country houses, as in The Destruction of the Country House exhibition at the Victoria and Albert Museum in 1974, but also in many articles about small British towns where modern architecture often seemed a force of blind destruction. After the expansiveness of the 1960s, there was a cycle of introspection and consolidation. This can be found architecturally expressed in houses such as Gorsfach, Gwynedd, by Alexander Potter, and Barley Splatt, Cornwall, by Martin Johnson and Graham Ovenden, both of which feel like an escape from the world.

During the 1980s, a defiant opposition to Modernism was still prevalent, but, despite an occasional reluctance on the part of owners to allow their new houses to appear in the magazine, *Country Life* continued to inform a wider public about architecture that was often well hidden in the depths of the countryside. Knowledge about post-war Classicism increased through John Cornforth's publication of three articles on Francis Johnson in 1984, and John Martin Robinson's piece on the otherwise unrecorded work of Bird and Tyler in 1989.

This might have been the end of the story, but quite early in the 1990s, the cycle turned once again. The decision made by the National Trust in 1991 to buy Ernö Goldfinger's No. 2 Willow Road showed, with perfect logic, that 'modern' could be 'heritage', even though the defence of earlier heritage had become one of the arguments against modern architecture. The history of pre-war Modernism had been studied by *Country Life* for some time, and was joined by a continuing review of post-war Modernism from 1993, when Farnley Hey became the first post-war Modernist house to be treated as historical. Since that time, the magazine has done much to affirm the quality and interest of post-war Modernism, revisiting houses that were also published when new, such as Peter Moro's in Blackheath, and adding houses that might have been published earlier but were not, such as No. 3 Church Walk, Aldeburgh. The imprimatur of *Country Life* has on several occasions helped to secure protection through listing, and a wide range of post-war houses, including Classical and modern examples, has been conserved in this way.

Meanwhile, new modern architecture began to appear again in the pages of *Country Life*. As in the 1930s and 1960s, there was no stylistic exclusiveness involved, and many architects were indeed still interested in finding a 'middle way' in what seemed a perennial battle of the styles, if only because most planning committees did not join in the favourable reappraisal of Modernism and often insisted on traditional materials and pitched roofs, even for houses whose intentions were more radical.

One change during the 1990s that in future will seem significant was the change in planning policy contained in a government document, called PPG7, introduced by John Gummer as Minister for Environment in 1996. This stated: 'An isolated new house in the countryside may

also exceptionally be justified if it is clearly of the highest quality, is truly outstanding in terms of its architecture and landscape design, and would significantly enhance its immediate setting and wider surroundings.' Several such houses have now been built, in both Classical and Modernist styles, although both kinds have met with local opposition, while a campaign has been started among architects to prevent the deletion of this clause from the next revision of the Planning Policy Guidance.

The justification given for altering the previous policy is very much in the spirit of *Country Life*'s commitment to the idea of a continuous tradition of domestic architecture in England, since it proposes that 'each generation would have the opportunity to add to the tradition of the Country House which has done so much to enhance the English countryside'.[19]

THE NEW HOUSE, SUSSEX (1984) Top: *John Outram's representative Post-Modernist house.*

BARLEY SPLATT, CORNWALL (1973) Above: *A design for Graham Ovenden's escapist fantasy, demonstrating a return to Gothic Revival.*

THE SPENDER STUDIO, MALDON, ESSEX (1968) Left: *Colour and wit bring life to an artist's modern house by Richard Rogers.*

ONE

FORGETTING THE FUTURE

1920-30

The 1920s has always been a difficult decade to categorise in British architecture. Much of the activity tends to look like a watered-down version of the Edwardian period, and the self-satisfaction expressed by writers of the time about the superiority of domestic architecture scarcely justified in the face of so much that seems timid and dull. Yet there are distinctive features among the houses illustrated here that indicate that new directions were being developed.

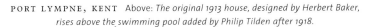

PORT LYMPNE, KENT   Above: *The original 1913 house, designed by Herbert Baker, rises above the swimming pool added by Philip Tilden after 1918.*

Left: *Rex Whistler painted the Tent Room in 1930, adding the final touch to the theatrical interiors.*

17

Port Lympne in Kent, a house that was built by Philip Sassoon to the designs of Herbert Baker before the First World War, and altered after 1918 by Philip Tilden (1887–1956), might offer a hypothesis about the nature of these new directions that can be tested on other examples from the decade. Baker had returned to Britain from a period of residence in South Africa in 1912, where he had built several houses in the Cape Dutch style. This was reflected in the shaped brick gables of Port Lympne, which was elevated on a bluff overlooking Romney Marsh, site of a former Roman port, from which the sea had retreated.

The main block remains much as Baker left it, but with only six bedrooms; Sassoon, heir to a considerable trading fortune from Shanghai, felt it was too small for the active life of political entertaining that he wished to embark on after the war, during which he had been secretary to General Earl Haig. Tilden's job was to enlarge Port Lympne and to make it, in his words, 'no more of the modest week-end home, but rather the epitome of all things conducive to luxurious relaxation after the strenuousness of war. It was to be a challenge to the world, telling people that a new culture had risen up from the sick-bed of the old, with new aspirations, eyes upon a new aspect, mind   ined to a new burst of imagination.'[1]

PORT LYMPNE, KENT Top: *The dining room, with 'lapis lazuli walls, gilt chairs with jade cushions, opalescent ceiling, and grey carpet'.*

Left: *The patio was created by Tilden on the roof of the service courtyard; it provided a spectacular outlook from the stairs.*

BRON-Y-DÊ, SURREY Above: *The house built by Philip Tilden for the Prime Minister, David Lloyd George, in 1920–21.*

In a period when country-house owners were more commonly dreaming of a past England, Port Lympne, inspired by the Roman history of the site, evoked dreams of almost anywhere else – Italy, Spain and Egypt in particular. Externally, Tilden's contribution was Classical in style and included the extraordinary flight of steps descending the hillside from the house to a marble-lined pool, the colonnaded quadrants that successfully enhance Baker's centre-piece, as well as a Classical triumph of arms carved in low relief in stone over the main entrance, complete with ancient Roman fasces.

Internally, Sassoon had already commissioned the Spanish painter José-Luis Sert (who was also employed by Serge Diaghilev to design sets and costumes for the Russian Ballet) to paint the drawing-room ceiling. Glyn Philpot painted the dining-room frieze in the Egyptian style, and in 1930 Rex Whistler, a new star in the world of mural painting, decorated the garden room with faux tenting and panoramas of an invented city, in a lighter style than that favoured by his predecessors. Under Tilden's hand, the central courtyard became a fantasy of Moorish Spain.

Sert completed the drawing-room walls in black and gold as an allegory of the war, although his work avoids direct reference to the unpleasantness of the actual event. If Edwardian taste was often opulent, Port Lympne was nothing less than theatrical. In seeking the exotic, it represented the strain of cultural inferiority in Britain that was later attracted to the Modern Movement. Sassoon was anxious to complete the first phase of alterations in order to hold an interna-tional conference between the British Prime Minister, Lloyd George, and the French Maréchal Foch, prior to the Versailles Peace Conference of 1919. *Country Life*'s article rose to the occasion, noting the subtle colour harmonies typical of 1920s decoration, which survive in very few houses and are sadly lost in black-and-white photography. Although occupying a pre-war shell, the interiors of Port Lympne, partly carried out by the decorating firm Baker and Wilmot, were relatively small in size, setting a new trend for detail rather than scale. The extravagant display of Port Lympne contrasts with Sassoon's

more conventional treatment of Trent Park, Hertfordshire, which he remodelled in an early-Georgian style.

A commission that came to Tilden directly as a result of Port Lympne was for a country house for Lloyd George himself, built rapidly on a ridge at Churt, Surrey, in 1920–21 and published in *Country Life* in 1922. To speed up construction, the house, called Bron-y-Dê ('facing south' in Welsh) had low brick walls with the upper storey in a mansard. To set an example to the nation, Lloyd George declared that despite the poor soil, he intended to farm the land and to make it pay, 'whatever it costs'. The style is much more restrained than at Port Lympne, and the house was modest in scale, although the study was built to the same dimensions as the Cabinet Room at Downing Street, in order that Lloyd George could pace up and down it with the same rhythm. By making additions and alterations to Chartwell for Winston Churchill in 1923–24, Tilden extended the range of his commissions for politicians still further.

If Port Lympne was theatrical, so, in a different way, was Coleton Fishacre in Devon, designed by Oswald Milne (1881–1967) for Rupert D'Oyly Carte, who had inherited several businesses from his father. These included the Savoy Hotel, the Savoy Theatre and the D'Oyly Carte Opera Company, still profitably performing the late-nineteenth-

COLETON FISHACRE, DEVON Top: *The entrance courtyard recalls the Edwardian Arts and Crafts movement at its simplest.*

Above: *The bedroom corridor makes an impressive vista, with tasselled light fittings.*

Right: *Oswald Milne designed a sheltered sitting space between the angle of the walls, with a smooth bow containing the study.*

century operettas of W. S. Gilbert and Arthur Sullivan. D'Oyly Carte first glimpsed the site, on the south Devon coast, from his yacht, and the house was constructed between 1923 and 1926. It stands at the head of a combe running down to the sea, in which a fine woodland garden was created by Lady Dorothy D'Oyly Carte.

Milne had been an assistant to Lutyens, but was more relaxed than his former master in his attitude to architectural form. Coleton makes a fine display of local stone walling and roof tiles, using the angled plan – known to the Edwardians as a 'butterfly plan' – to good effect to create an entrance courtyard with fine radiating granite paving, and a sheltered terrace facing the garden and views of the sea. All this is soberly Arts and Crafts, though streamlined in its horizontal emphasis. The theatricality begins indoors, not on anything like the scale of Port Lympne, but using some of the same means of colour and exoticism, with the imitation-lapis-lazuli dining table, the Lalique dining-room lights and light fittings in the corridors with a mixture of real and imitation tassels.

The Paris Exhibition of Industrial and Modern Decorative Art took place in 1925, at the point when the furnishing of Coleton Fishacre would have been under consideration. The Art Deco style, which allowed for decoration without definite historical reference, later took its name from this event. Coleton displays the characteristic Art Deco mixture of broad masculine shapes with feminine details. Lady Dorothy D'Oyly Carte had a Raoul Dufy fabric in her bedroom, and bathroom tiles came from Carter's of Poole to designs by Edward Bawden, who exhibited in Paris as a student. Around 1930, the American designer Marion Dorn, known as 'the architect of floors' for her specialisation in one-off rugs, designed a series of rugs for the drawing room at Coleton in pale green and cream; these have

COUR, ARGYLLSHIRE Above: *The sense of scale of Oliver Hill's first major house is deceptive, for the house is not as big as it looks. Features such as the pepperpot turrets add to its Scottish character.*

Right: *Oliver Hill camped for two weeks on the estate to find the best position for the house, on the eastern side of Kintyre overlooking Kilbrannan Sound.*

COUR, ARGYLLSHIRE Above: *The main staircase is massive, simple, and filled with light.*

Left: *A wide door beneath a deep arch leads from the Great Hall on to a terrace. The walls are built of local whinstone.*

remained in the house and are now in the care of the National Trust. The rugs create atmosphere in a room whose three semicircular steps down from the door allow for a dramatic entry.

It is interesting to move from Coleton to Cour, Argyllshire, a house of 1922 by Oliver Hill (1887–1968) on the eastern side of Kintyre, looking across Kilbrannan Sound to the Isle of Arran, built for John Braidwood Gray, a Glasgow-born shipping insurance broker. Photographs and drawings of Cour were exhibited and published, and may therefore have influenced Milne's design of Coleton. Although unsuccessful in his attempt to become a pupil of Lutyens, Hill was a passionate admirer of his work; however, like Coleton, Cour is in no way a pastiche of Lutyens. The greatest resemblance to Lutyens is in the trick of scale by which the entrance front is smaller than one might expect, enhancing its apparent size and distance from the

approach drive. The external doors are both wider and lower than normal. There are more salient features, such as the pepperpot turrets with traditional Scottish ogival roofs. Hill's family came from Aberdeen, and he had fought in the war with the London Scottish Regiment; he had a bullet-marked kilt to prove it.

The plan is L-shaped, with a comfortable internal angle to catch the morning sun. The detailing is very simple, but all the openings, whether of windows or supporting walls in the corridor leading from the drawing room to the dining room, are arched, as if to avoid the harshness of right angles. The bedrooms extend dramatically upwards into the roof space. There was no way of hiding the service areas of the house in such an exposed position, and Hill made a good feature of the kitchen courtyard by placing it next to the tall mullioned bay of the stair window.

Cour was Hill's first major construction, although he had altered houses and created gardens before the war. He spent two weeks on the site to absorb the feeling of the landscape before deciding where to place the house, and it was built, like Coleton Fishacre, from stone quarried on the estate. This was the only major house by Hill not to

appear in *Country Life*; the omission was rectified in 1992, when the house, although in need of repair, remained inhabited and architecturally unaltered.

Cour and Coleton may appear almost 'modern' in their simplicity, even though their materials and construction techniques were traditional. As much as Port Lympne, however, they indicate a complex relationship with the past that during the 1920s took on a multitude of different forms. One of these was the trade in architectural antiques and the re-erection of parts of buildings. These were relatively inexpensive, and Lutyens set a precedent when in 1910 he persuaded Nathaniel Lloyd to buy the timber frame of a derelict hall house and move it 9 miles from Benenden to Great Dixter, to be incorporated into an existing house of similar date. Today such practices would be doubly condemned: for removing one building from its context and diminishing the legibility and authenticity of another, but it would have been seen at the time as a virtuous act of rescue.

Hammels, at Boars Hill in Oxfordshire, a location much favoured by Oxford academics for building new houses high above the university town, was built around the frame of a barn moved from Hertfordshire, which, like many agricultural buildings across the

HAMMELS, OXFORDSHIRE Top: *The barn fills the right-hand end of the house. The client was a professor of horticulture at Oxford, and there was an elaborate garden plan.*

Above: *The library is made of elm, the use of which was revived after the First World War owing to shortage of other timbers.*

Left: *The living room is made from the timbers of a Herefordshire barn, creating the Tudor look popular in the 1920s.*

OARE HOUSE, WILTSHIRE Above: *The library added in 1925 by Clough Williams-Ellis for Sir Geoffrey Fry, in his fashionably simplified and elongated Georgian style. The Baroque curves of the hanging lights are influenced by Swedish Classical design of the 1920s.*

HARROWILL COPSE, SURREY Below: *This small house, combining Classical and vernacular elements, was built on the estate of Williams-Ellis's father-in-law. The architect built an almost identical house, Cold Blow, at Oare for Geoffrey Fry.*

country, had fallen into disuse. The client was Sir Frederick Keeble, a professor of horticulture, and the architects were G. Blair Imrie and T. G. Angell.

The barn made a fine double-height living room, at one end of a long rectangular plan with a single roof-line, simply composed on the garden front with elm weatherboarding and a single projecting square bay. The entrance front is more varied, but in the *Country Life* article of 1923, Randal Phillips assured readers that the design had been steered by economics rather than a conscious desire for Picturesqueness. Indeed, compared to many other houses evoking pre-Tudor England, Hammels shares the design discipline of Baillie-Scott or Voysey of twenty years before. Imrie and Angell are relatively unknown, although they built a great many houses, including clusters of well-considered pre-1914 surburban houses at West Byfleet in Surrey.[2]

Inside Hammels, there were numerous touches typical of the 1920s. Lady Keeble may have been the aesthete of the couple, who displayed a painting of the Crucifixion by Charles Ricketts in the living room and various Baroque candlesticks and lanterns with tassels, giving 'a bright note of colour'. Her own bedroom is described as failing to conform to any particular style, 'furniture and decorative features of different kinds, both old and new, English and foreign, being mingled'. On a much quieter level, this was the same principle of eclectic inclusion seen at Port Lympne. As at Coleton Fishacre, the exterior was the sober, masculine aspect of the house, and the interior more playfully feminine.

At the end of the 1930s, the cartoonist Osbert Lancaster produced a pair of books that have remained unmatched in their invention of stylistic categories for the inter-war years. *Pillar to Post* (1938) described the exteriors of buildings from Stonehenge to the present, and *Homes Sweet Homes* (1939) was a companion volume dealing with interiors. Hammels would qualify as a mixture of 'Stockbroker's Tudor' and 'Curzon Street Baroque', the latter being a smart society style as its name implies, based on the amassing of foreign bric-à-brac, often of ecclesiastical origin.

The supreme master of Curzon Street Baroque was Clough Williams-Ellis (1883–1978), an architect whose practice, like Oliver Hill's, had been established just before the First World War, in which he had served gallantly in the tank regiment. Marrying into the Strachey family, Williams-Ellis became a mixture of architectural jester and deadly serious campaigner for the preservation of British landscape and buildings. His preference was for Classicism, but he chose simplified, naïve and sketchy forms of it, like the illustrations and stage sets by Claud Lovat Fraser that were so popular at the beginning of the 1920s.

Williams-Ellis was prolific, but built few big houses. One of his most widely published works of the 1920s was Oare House, Wiltshire, a 1770s house to which he added a library and ballroom wing for Sir Geoffrey Fry, inheritor of the Fry's chocolate fortune and private secretary to Stanley Baldwin, three-times prime minister between 1924 and 1938. This was the age of dance crazes, and

Williams-Ellis himself won several commissions through his skill on the dance floor.

In 1922, Fry built a smaller house on his estate, a thatched-roof design by Williams-Ellis with a compact plan, called Cold Blow. This was widely illustrated as a model for a modest house. He also designed a rather patrician row of cottages for agricultural workers in Oare village. At other locations, such as Cornwell in Oxfordshire in 1939, Williams-Ellis recreated the role of a Georgian 'estate architect': restoring cottages, infilling with new buildings and adding a village hall, all picturesquely grouped around a watersplash, as a demonstration of seemly and unified development. His main testament to sensitive development was Portmeirion, a hotel in the form of an Italianate village begun in 1926 on his own land in North Wales.

The quality of archness found in Williams-Ellis's work may indicate the mixture of relief and anxiety felt at the end of the war, when it was difficult to know whether to laugh or cry at the state of the world. As Martin Green and John Swan have written in *The Triumph of*

Pierrot, the tradition of the Italian Commedia dell'Arte provided a set of images and attitudes interwoven with the culture of Modernism in Europe from 1900 onwards, in which architecture and decoration increasingly resembled stage scenery. At Port Lympne, the disjunction between the character of the different rooms was like a series of contrasting scenes at a play. The apparently backward-looking nature of virtually all 1920s houses in Britain, which has put them out of the range of interest for many historians, can perhaps be understood in more subtle ways as a response to the very specific conditions of the time. Although the 1930s brought a more obvious form of Modernism, which for some offered a welcome end to the masquerade of styles, a great number of houses of the 1930s continued the themes of the previous decade with little evidence of interruption.

Edwin Lutyens (1869–1944), the vigorous survivor from an earlier period of domestic architecture, could be called as a witness in support of the transitions of the 1920s. He built fewer houses after 1920 than before the First World War, evidence perhaps of a general slowdown. With the footprint of the house extended to include a forecourt of service buildings, a house such as Gledstone Hall, Yorkshire (see page 7), strives after an effect of grand Classical scale without actually being larger than his earlier works. Compared to the

fireworks of his early work, the later houses seem compact and undemonstrative, rather in the way that one of John Galsworthy's characters in *The Forsyte Saga* described Lutyens' Cenotaph as 'a monument to the dread of swank'. Only perhaps at the more informal Plumpton Place, Lutyens' final commission for Edward Hudson, the founder and owner of *Country Life*, did some of the old warmth return.

Lutyens built two further houses of significance in the 1930s, which continue similar themes. No. 42 Cheyne Walk, London, built in 1930, was a wedding present to Mrs Guy Liddell (née Calypso Baring) from her father, Lord Revelstoke, for whom Lutyens had altered and enlarged Lambay Castle at the beginning of the century. It was an extraordinary London house, which as *Country Life* observed, was more like a country house in town, set back from the Chelsea Embankment because the site opened up behind a narrow frontage.

The commentary by A. S. G. Butler on this design in the *Lutyens Memorial* volumes (published by *Country Life* Books in 1950) is instructive, for it helps one to see the amount of calculation that went into the plan and elevation of even a simple-looking house like this. Butler noted that only one window on the south front, the one in the gable, is a conventionally proportioned double-hung sash. The others are either wider or narrower, thus avoiding monotony. In plan, the central spine, parallel with the front elevation and dividing the main set of rooms on the front from less formal ones behind, appears to be nearly 3 feet thick, allowing for flues, deep doorways and cupboards, and concealed pipework. The external walls are also unusually massive, giving the effect of deep window reveals typical of older houses. These kinds of modifications, the extra cost of which Lutyens was adept at charming out of his clients, helped make the difference between an exceptional house and an unexceptional one in a way that is not apparent to the casual observer.

Butler also commented on Lutyens' innovative skill, in all his houses, at hiding all the external rainwater downpipes, soil pipes and vent pipes required by the building regulations on the outside of the building. He gained concessions from building inspectors in order to be allowed to run these all inside the walls, an effect that other architects then aspired to copy.

Inside No. 42 Cheyne Walk, Lutyens produced some of his most 'amusing' decorative effects, many with unconventional forms of wallpaper, from the French landscape paper (newly fashionable in 1930) similar in effect to a Rex Whistler mural in the day nursery, blue marble paper in the nursery dining room, travel posters in the servants' sitting room and pictureless pages from the newly redesigned *Times* newspaper in the servants' corridor.

For other architects, Lutyens' influence was hard to escape. W. Curtis Green (1875–1960) had roots in the Arts and Crafts movement, as Lutyens also did, and was in some respects a more careful Classicist; but he won a limited competition for a large country house, Stockgrove Park, Bedfordshire, in 1928, for F. M. Kroyer-Kielberg, with a design that was a composite of Lutyens motifs, also built with a forecourt. This was not published in *Country Life* until 1939, when

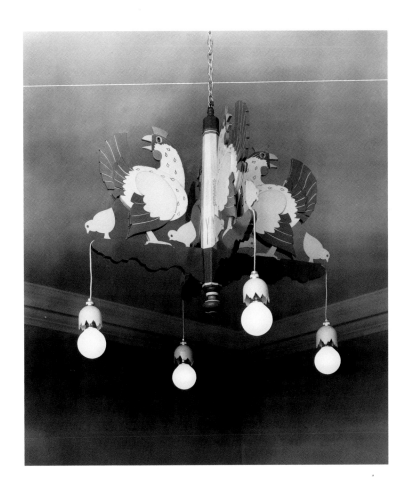

NO. 42 CHEYNE WALK, LONDON *Top: Startled hens hatch light-bulb eggs in a joke light fitting for the night nursery.*

Above: *Travel posters make wallpaper for the servants' sitting room.*

Left: *The stone staircase achieves drama even inside a small house.*

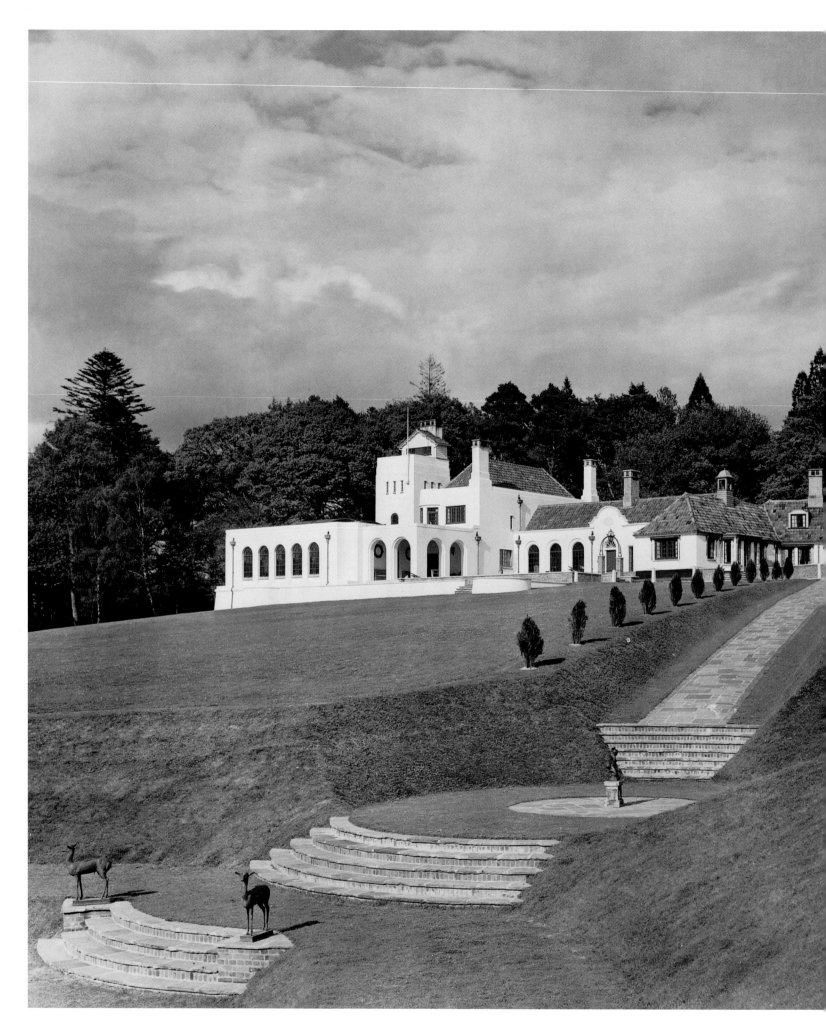

Arthur Oswald politely stressed the building's 'homely informal Englishness', with its deliberate avoidance of monumentality which undoubtedly makes the overall composition seem disappointing, more fitting perhaps for its later institutional use, first as a wartime hospital and then as a Camden Council boarding school in the second half of the century. The 80-foot vaulted swimming bath attached to one of the wings seems to have predicted such a future.

Swimming baths and squash courts began to be incorporated in houses during the 1920s as the upper classes took to sunbathing and the cult of the body. Woodfalls, Hampshire, designed by Braddell and Deane, was built in two phases between 1928 and 1930 for the Hon. Henry Mond, the son of one of the founders of ICI, in the grounds of the family home, Melchett Park. His wife, Gwen Mond, a quint-essential figure of the 1920s with her mysterious past, her slender figure and cropped red hair, was worried about the tubercular glands of her two younger children, and built them a bungalow with easy access to a garden, at a distance from the main house.

The Monds had enjoyed acting as architectural patrons in their London house in Westminster, and in 1929, after Henry Mond had spent the summer convalescing in the bungalow, he decided to enlarge it. It remained the equivalent of those miniature houses to which European royalty might retire from worldly cares. The exterior was in a Mediterranean vernacular style, Picturesquely assembled. The largest room was the pool, a magnificent Roman creation with green *scagliola* columns and heated water with underwater lighting for Mrs Mond's midnight bathes. While suggesting future informality of lifestyle, Woodfalls remained within the conventions of domestic architecture.

WOODFALLS, HAMPSHIRE Above: *The swimming bath, seen here from outside, was the largest room in the house, but its bulk is set off by the tower behind, giving an intentionally nautical effect with the porthole windows and white-painted walls.*

Left: *The first part of the house, to the right, was designed by Braddell and Deane to provide healthy living conditions for the Mond children. Their parents enjoyed being there so much that they extended it into a luxurious bungalow.*

The house of the architect Sir Edward Maufe (1883–1974) and his wife, Prudence, at Shepherd's Hill, Sussex, was a reconstruction of a farmhouse adjoining a fine stable block built in 1740, which provides an entrance archway linked to the house beyond with an ingenious combination of architectural and landscape features. Created between 1926 and 1928, Shepherd's Hill was recognised as a valuable survival of the 1920s when John Cornforth described it in *Country Life* in 1975, shortly before Lady Maufe's death and the sale of its contents. Having launched his career with a large country house, Kelling Hall, Norfolk, in 1912, Maufe was a rising star of the 1920s, who added the influence of contemporary Swedish design to his Arts and Crafts roots, as seen in the silver-leaf furniture that he exhibited in the British Pavilion at the Paris Exhibition of 1925, now in the Victoria and Albert Museum.

Prudence Maufe worked at Heal's, the London furnishing store, from 1916 until 1971, influencing the taste of thousands of middle-class customers by gradually introducing occasional touches of chromed steel among the limed oak and oatmeal fabrics, so that by the late 1930s Modernism was seen as an acceptable style. Colour schemes and textures rather than new shapes were the key to the Maufes' work at Shepherd's Hill, and carefully selected antiques, including a Venetian Baroque mirror and a seventeenth-century tapestry in the main bedroom, were easily accommodated.

Maufe's style usually involved placing a decorative detail against a plain background, as seen in the projecting entrance porch of Shepherd's Hill, with its carved relief by Eric Gill of a coat of arms and three nude figures. Another Gill sculpture was placed in a niche in the dining room, forming the centrepiece of a composition of steps, chrome handrails and arched openings. In this room, the brick was painted rather than plastered, and the ceiling painted blue to match the curtains. Where Clough Williams-Ellis might have exaggerated the colours for effect, Maufe softened and harmonised, as evoked by John Cornforth in his description of the drawing room: 'The walls of roughened plaster and the ceiling are both painted a soft pink, and tones throughout the room are rose, stone-coloured velvet for the curtains and off-white for the carpet on the dry-rubbed floor. Bold and complicated patterns are avoided, and there used to be even fewer pictures breaking up the areas of wall.'[3]

This is a difficult style to recreate in real life or in imagination, for few actual examples survive intact. Maufe's religious buildings, such as St Saviour's, Acton (1924–26), and Guildford Cathedral (1932–61), can still give an impression of his style, complete with silver candle-sticks and specially woven textiles.

The first house in Britain that can be described as Modernist, owing to its cubic shape, flat roof, white walls and horizontal emphasis, was New Ways, Northampton, designed in 1925 by the German architect Peter Behrens for W. Bassett-Lowke, a local

WOODFALLS, HAMPSHIRE *No indoor pool of the inter-war period was more dreamlike than that of Woodfalls, with its black-marble bath, green columns and gold capitals. A brass seahorse spouts water from the church-like apse at the far end.*

industrialist. Within a few years, other houses of similar appearance began to be built. There was a growing interest in the writings of Le Corbusier, notably his book, *Vers une architecture*, published in 1923 and translated into English in 1927, partly because it provided good material for the popular press.

In *Decline and Fall*, his first novel (1927), Evelyn Waugh describes a new house on an historic site called King's Thursday. This has been built by the wealthy socialite Margot Beste-Chetwynd with the help of a German architect, Professor Otto Silenus, who advocates an architecture based on a machine aesthetic, devoid of historical reference or human emotion. Historians have searched for the originals of Professor Silenus and King's Thursday, but at the time of the book's publication, nothing so extreme actually existed in Britain, although one might trace the rhetoric back to Le Corbusier and the physical form to examples such as the Villa Noailles at Hyères by Robert Mallet-Stevens, the first part of which was built in 1924.

British observers of the 'New Architecture' abroad preferred to believe the caricature version, so evidently typical of foreign extremism and intellectualism, although they were occasionally reminded that the style was derived from the English Arts and Crafts movement.

SHEPHERD'S HILL, SUSSEX Top: *An alcove in the dining room houses Eric Gill's sculpture* Headdress *(1928), which was set on a turntable so that the viewing angle could be altered.*

Above: *In the main bedroom, a seventeenth-century tapestry looms large beside a tiered chimneypiece in the style of Daniel Marot.*

Left: *The tower at the entrance to Sir Edward Maufe's house has a Scottish character, which may have derived from Maufe's collection of paintings by the artist James Pryde.*

Oliver Hill is one of the most interesting architects to observe as he moved from the historically based architecture of Cour to become, in some projects at least, a complete Modernist in the 1930s. His range included a thatched, half-timbered style and a Neo-Georgian style. He did not insist on accurate historical detail, but his understanding of building materials and craft techniques was good enough to ensure that even if his houses often looked like stage sets, they had a satisfactory physical reality. The belief that rooms should offer scope for fantasy and invention made the transition from Baroque or Oriental taste into Modernism an easy one. Smart London hostesses picked up the fashion for Modernism, and Hill was one of the designers who was happy to make interiors that would be certain to attract attention. Materials such as plate glass and chrome steel, which in the imagination of some architects were the means of forging a new architecture for the masses, were more often to be found as playthings for the rich.

Lady Mount Temple, whose politician husband was Minister of Transport in Ramsay MacDonald's Labour government, was an enthusiast for house decoration and had collaborated with several professional decorating firms; she also ran Flower Decorations, a florist's catering to the new mania for flower arrangements. She first employed Oliver Hill in 1926 to design a town house in Gayfere Street, near the church of St John in London's Smith Square, an area of small early-Georgian houses that was becoming fashionable, particularly for MPs. Henry and Gwen Mond were only a few doors away at Mulberry House, where they created a drawing room with a bas-relief entitled *Scandal* by the sculptor C. S. Jagger over the fireplace, and stylised murals by Glyn Philpot of Oedipus and the Sphynx, among other mythological episodes.[4] The first Gayfere House had a drawing room covered in gold leaf, an effect that Oliver Hill had first seen at Tofts Manor, Bedfordshire, in a room decorated by the artist James McNeill Whistler, and the 'undersea' bathroom he created became instantly famous.

In 1929, Oliver Hill planned a second house for Lord and Lady Mount Temple, only a short distance away, confusingly also called

GAYFERE HOUSE, LONDON (1929) *Above: Furnished with elaborate simplicity, the little sitting room was a collaboration between Oliver Hill and his client, Lady Mount Temple. The hearth is made of black mirror and the shutters geometrically patterned in white and green.*

Right: Ceramic cats guard the stairs beneath a peach-coloured mirror ceiling. The mixture of modern decoration with historically derived furniture, like the dining-room table seen beyond the doorway, was typical of this transitional phase of Modernism.

Gayfere House. It was in fact part of a development of four houses, including North House for the MP Robert Hudson, which received a more restrained decorative treatment. The outside was Neo-Georgian, but inside Gayfere House it was another matter, and, as *Country Life* reported, the architect and client were 'free to criticise and protest, though each undertook not to destroy anything original in the work of the other'.

The magazine also noted that the ancient art of China, brought to public attention by some major acquisitions at the British Museum in the early years of the century, was a strong influence on the paring-down of detail and clutter. As the article went on to say, 'there is nothing in the traditions of Western taste to account for the modern delight in empty spaces that are yet "composed" by means of a few aptly placed objects; for the introduction of a single spray of flowers as the key of a decorative scheme; or the harmonious combination of

wayward lines into a satisfying unity'.[5] It was as much a reversion to the Oriental taste of the Aesthetic Movement in the 1870s as a commitment to something of recent invention.

New building materials did play a part at Gayfere House, with peach-coloured mirror glass on the ceiling of the entrance hall, where the rest of the scheme consisted of laminated shell-pink myrtle wood, stainless steel, and black- and cream-coloured marble forming the alternating treads of the staircase – a trick stolen from Lutyens, who used it at Gledstone Hall in 1926. The walls were combed vertically in Plastex paint. The tall staircase window was glazed with opaque glass and had its own built-in electric lighting so that it would glow in the night.

The dramatic bathroom, with its walls and ceiling covered in dark-grey mirror, was described in one of the newspapers as 'Lady Mount Temple's Crystal Palace'. The colour scheme was extended with pieces of blue glass displayed on shelves, gold mosaic in the bath and golden-yellow towels.

GAYFERE HOUSE, LONDON (1929) Above: *With green glazed walls, and 'a bed set in a crystal alcove and resting on crystal feet' standing on a 'milk-white floor', the colours and textures of Lady Mount Temple's bedroom, combined with zebra hide, created 'the elegant fantasy of a fairy-tale of Perrault'.*

Left: *The small space of the bathroom was multiplied by dark-grey mirrors on walls and ceiling. It was described as 'a chef d'œuvre of bagnotechnica'.*

TWO

BUILDING POLITICS

1930-40

In *Nobody Talks Politics* (1936), Geoffrey Gorer described how a young man at a party at an English university in 1924 is bitten by a lemur and wakes up, like Rip van Winkle, after being asleep for ten years. During this time, the social conversation has changed from gossip and aesthetics to politics and almost nothing else. As in previous ages, much of the discussion about politics took place in the setting of private houses, particularly over weekends. Architecture was politicised too, with a 'battle of the styles' between traditional and modern.

ELTHAM PALACE, LONDON Above: *Mah-Jong, the pet ring-tailed lemur, lived in a specially decorated and heated cage.*

HIGH AND OVER, BUCKINGHAMSHIRE Left: *Amyas Connell's creation of a roof garden for the benefit of the Ashmoles' children answered one of Le Corbusier's Five Points of a New Architecture.*

Early in the new decade, *Country Life* readers were introduced by Christopher Hussey to the first major house in England to be built in the style of the European Modern Movement: High and Over, at Amersham, a small town in Buckinghamshire within easy commuting distance of London, commissioned by Professor Bernard Ashmole. He was a Classical archaeologist who had recently returned from a spell as director of the British School at Rome. Among the architects at the school was Amyas Connell (1901–80), originally from New Zealand, who, in addition to fulfilling his duties in measuring and drawing out Classical and Renaissance monuments, had become entranced with the new European theories that sought to rediscover the essential tenets of architecture. In Le Corbusier's *Vers une architecture*, the best-known text on the subject, his combination of liners, cars and aeroplanes with Greek temples suggested that modern civilisation was in direct continuity with antiquity.

HIGH AND OVER, BUCKINGHAMSHIRE Above: *The house is designed with three wings joined at the centre. The formal garden, designed by the architect, extends the geometry of the house in the manner of French Cubist gardens of the 1920s.*

Left: *The staircase winds up inside a glazed turret next to the double-height hall. The fountain jet from the central pool below was capable of rising to the level of the first-floor balcony.*

The Ashmoles' original concept for High and Over was an E-plan house of Elizabethan derivation. Having found their site, on the edge of an old chalkpit on a hillside, they changed this to a splayed design, familiar from Edwardian practice, but made geometrically tighter around a central hexagonal entrance hall. The architect's contribution to the interiors showed awareness of contemporary fashions for glass and metal finishes, especially in the living room, with its shiny jade-green cellulose spray paint and its chromium steel trim around the fireplace. At the centre of the staircase hall was a fountain inset into the floor and lit from below, one of several poetic evocations of the Mediterranean. The nursery was on the top floor, so that the children could use the flat roof as a playing space. From here, it was possible to look down on Connell's garden design in the French Cubist style, with its strongly demarcated geometrical compartments for planting and a deliberately 'unnatural' effect.

The next modern house to receive a full article by Hussey was High Cross House at Dartington, Devon, in 1933, described as 'probably the most extreme instance in England of the functional type of house associated with the name of Le Corbusier'. The architect, William Lescaze (1896–1969), was Swiss in origin like Le Corbusier, but practised in America with William Howe. The house was built for

the incoming headmaster of Dartington School, W. B. Curry, who, although English, had been head of a progressive school at Croton-on-Hudson in New York State, designed by Lescaze and funded by the conductor Leopold Stokowski.

The money behind the Dartington experiment in rural regeneration and education was American, inherited by Dorothy Elmhirst, who had chosen Devon as the site for the project dreamed up by her English husband, Leonard, who in turn had been inspired by the teaching and example of the Bengali poet Rabindranath Tagore. Dartington, in short, was International in flavour, while also rooted to the beautiful and ancient house and garden bought by the Elmhirsts in 1926. Prospective headmaster Curry persuaded the Dartington Hall Trust to dispense with their existing architect, Oswald Milne, since he argued that only a Modernist like Lescaze could build a house that exploited scientific ideas of living to the full – Curry being a scientist himself.

Because of the transatlantic correspondence required to secure Lescaze's appointment, more than the usual amount of detail survives to account for Dartington's conversion to Modernism. Curiously, the aesthetics of the cubic house with a flat roof, which provide the enduring impression of High Cross, were hardly mentioned at all. Instead, the argument was based on the relatively spurious grounds of practicality and economy, but this was typical of the polemical attitude of Modernism, which excluded aesthetic rationale lest this suggest the involvement of personal taste rather than demonstrable fact. If High and Over could be explained more as a return to a purer Classicism than as a revolution, then High Cross could only be explained as an essay in pure form. Hussey found 'the resulting simplicity decidedly refreshing', since, in common with other

HIGH CROSS HOUSE, DEVON Above and left: *With its smooth rendered surfaces, metal windows, roof terraces, projecting balconies, and streamlined curved corner, the house represents the characteristics of the International Style of modern architecture, named after an exhibition held in New York in 1932, the year of its completion. The darker-toned section of the building was painted cobalt blue.*

proponents of Modernism, he made a distinction between the 'real' modern and 'the pseudo and "arty" ', which we would today recognise as Art Deco.[1]

Like High and Over, High Cross was a large house, planned in 1930 before money grew tighter, even though Dartington was well cushioned against economic reality. Despite Lescaze's claims for scientific planning, the use of space is extravagant. The modern construction proved difficult for local builders, and, with an architect far away, was long drawn out and expensive. The flat roof leaked, but Lescaze went on to build more for Dartington School and for the estate with greater physical success and economy. In exterior composition, the house lacks the skill of a more experienced architect (such as Erich Mendelsohn, who settled in England as a refugee from Germany in 1933), but since its restoration by John Winter in 1995, High Cross has regained the blue paint originally applied to one of its

cubic volumes in an effect based on the Dutch De Stijl movement. Today, it houses the collections and archives of the Dartington Trust. Hussey quoted Bill Curry's endorsement that as occupier he 'always came back to it with a real sense of relief after having visited a more old-fashioned house crowded with furniture and knick-knacks'.[2]

For those who believe that *Country Life* reflects conservative attitudes, the serious consideration of modern houses such as High Cross, by an aesthete such as Christopher Hussey, may seem surprising. Yet while Connell and Lescaze would have disdained designing anything except a modern house at this time, the magazine was more widely inclusive and therefore provides a balanced record of the period. If Modernism sometimes appears in the guise of a great white foreign bird alighting suddenly in England, there were home-bred varieties representing an accumulation of artistic experience and philosophy.

Other architects occupied a variety of middle positions in relation to Modernism, however, and Hussey's texts describing their houses indicate that he set wider criteria for appropriate design. In June 1933, five months after the publication of High Cross, Hussey wrote about Yaffle Hill, a house at Broadstone, near Poole Harbour in Dorset, built for Cyril Carter, a manufacturer whose locally made Poole

Pottery and Carter's Tiles had been recognised as making fresh contributions to design since the First World War. The architect was Sir Edward Maufe, whose design, in Hussey's words, afforded 'all the amenities of a modern functional dwelling – a large area of glass, flat roofs for sleeping, and facilities for throwing the principal rooms open to the air, without departing from the traditional conception of a house, with roof, chimneys and a balanced ration of voids to solids'.[3] He noted the similarity of the splayed plan with High and Over, and the play of geometry and shiny surfaces also tells of the early stages of Modernism in Britain.

The rooms at Yaffle Hill were carefully furnished with pieces from Heal's, and the photographs taken for *Country Life* were often reproduced in books on interiors of the period. Only the original colours, including greys, blacks and yellows, are missing, although Carter's own pottery provided bright-blue tiles for the roofs, a

YAFFLE HILL, DORSET Above: *The exterior is more conservative than the interior, with its Mediterranean blue tiled roofs and arches.*

Left: *The splayed plan resembles High and Over, but the Art Deco character of the staircase, with its jade-green handrail, is more apparent. The tile mosaic picturing the house, by the client's own company, Carter's Tiles, is visible on the hall floor.*

decorative mosaic for the entrance hall, and a modelled 'yaffle' or woodpecker over the entrance, all of which remain *in situ*.

Ashcombe Tower, near Dawlish in Devon, was designed by Brian O'Rorke (1901–74) for Ralph Rayner. The siting of the house was politically motivated, since Rayner built it in order to have a base in his constituency on becoming MP for the Totnes Division. It was also unusual in being the centre of a newly created farming estate of 2,000 acres. Rayner was married to Elizabeth Courtauld, whose family had made a clever investment in viscose rayon before the First World War and thus prospered while the rest of Britain's textile industry declined. O'Rorke was chosen by Mrs Rayner on the grounds that he had never designed such a house before and would therefore be open to her ideas, but his name had subsequently become well known on account of his interiors for the Orient Line ship *Orion*, launched in 1934, the year that Ashcombe Tower was completed.

The rooms are relatively few, but they are spacious and well lit, with a wide opening between the drawing room (called 'The Big Room' on plans) and dining room, making it ideal for entertaining. These rooms still maintain their specially designed curtains and rugs by Marion Dorn, in which colour and texture are both emphasised. Textiles were a key aspect of furnishing in the inter-war period, and

only rarely survive. The dining room has cherry-red curtains with lines of white tufting and high-backed leather chairs in the same colour, with much use of mirrors and decorative stars on the built-in sideboard and side tables. It is a festive, frivolous room. The fireplace in the Big Room is set into a recess with lowered ceiling and raised floor, an intimate space in which the nation's problems might be discussed late at night.

The exterior of Ashcombe, built around an old viewing tower on the site, is by contrast underplayed, with broad slate roofs and rather narrow quoins of local limestone set into the rendered walls. Novelties include a cocktail bar under the stair, a built-in squash court, and pennies of King George V plated in silver as centres to the handles on the double entrance doors.

During the same period that Ashcombe Tower was under construction, Stephen Courtauld, a cousin of Mrs Rayner, was planning a

YAFFLE HILL, DORSET Above and right: *The study makes good use of a projecting wall (housing the garage on the other side), to enclose a sofa with bookcase fitments. The careful detailing continues through the other bookcases. The walls were painted warm grey and the ceiling yellow. The floor was made of Korkoid rubber in black, grey and yellow.*

Left: *The visitors' bathroom is tiled in scarlet, black and white on a background of beige mosaic.*

ASHCOMBE TOWER, DEVON Top: *The house was built on to an eighteenth-century tower, which was adapted by Brian O'Rorke for the Rayner family and completed in 1934.*

Above: *The staircase has an unusual timber balustrade, with junctions emphasised by steel bolts. In the stairwell, a cocktail bar is concealed beneath the half-landing.*

Right: *The living room retains original rugs and curtains by Marion Dorn. The dining room is seen beyond.*

more complex project in the suburbs of south-east London. Eltham Palace was one of the royal palaces of the late Middle Ages, of which a Great Hall commissioned by Edward IV was the main surviving part. Courtauld took a fifty-year lease from the Crown on Eltham and its extensive grounds in 1933, as the lease on his town house in Grosvenor Square was ending and he wanted to create a large garden in an area still convenient for reaching central London. Even today, the suburban development surrounding Eltham Palace disappears as one crosses the moat and catches sight of the distant views towards London.

The whole creation is romantic and improbable, with a new wing attached to the original hall designed by the young architects John Seely (1901–63) and Paul Paget (1901–85) in a French Renaissance style, but containing interiors in a wide variety of styles, mostly by the decorator, the Marchese Malacrida. The entrance leads into a circular hall, decorated with marquetry designs of Venice and Stockholm, with representative neo-medieval armed men standing guard, and a circular rug by Marion Dorn in a completely different abstract style. From this hinge point on the plan, one wing connects with the Great Hall, which the Courtaulds repaired and furnished, and contains the drawing room, library and boudoir, while the other contains the dining room and the service accommodation. These are all large rooms, the dining room in a smooth, European form of abstracted Classicism, the drawing room a rather Hollywood-style recreation of Renaissance Italy, deemed suitable for the display of Old Master paintings.

Perhaps Eltham was intended to register more as a sumptuous private museum than as a house, although Stephen Courtauld's collecting was modest compared to that of his cousin, Samuel, the founder of the Courtauld Institute of Art. Stephen's English water-colours were displayed in his study, with sliding panels to protect them from the light. He commissioned the sculptor Gilbert Ledward to carve stone decorations for the exterior, and to create a series of relief panels for the drawing-room window reveals, based on themes from Oswald Spengler's book *The Decline of the West*. In a niche on the outside of his squash court, Courtauld installed a heroic bronze of St George by Alfred Hardiman, who, like Ledward, was a Rome Scholar in sculpture. This figure had originally stood in a similar niche in Carlos Place, off Grosvenor Square.

Other iconography is teasingly scattered through the house at Eltham, and it is not clear whether it adds up to a complete theme. Whimsicality seems rather to prevail, as was certainly the case with Mah-Jong, a pet lemur that might have given Geoffrey Gorer the idea for his book, since he was apt to nip unwary guests' fingers when he descended the bamboo ladder from his centrally heated upstairs room.

The term 'Art Deco' became popular in the late 1960s, and it is one convenient label for the many versions of Modernism between the wars that were theatrical or decorative. In Britain, it was initially seen as a French style, although American interpretations of the original French sources became more influential in the 1930s. Veneered

surfaces, which are a feature of the interiors at Eltham, were one typical aspect of the style, although the most American characteristic of the interiors, reminiscent of William Randoph Hearst's castle of San Simeon on a reduced scale, is their mixture of styles and combination of reproduction with genuine antiques.

Although Christopher Hussey never let fall his mask of politeness, one suspects that he found Eltham rather vulgar. Contrasting the present with the reign of Charles II, when Sir John Shaw built the nearby Eltham Lodge in a pure Classical style, Hussey wrote that 'it is significant of the eclectic taste of our own time that the house now under consideration ... comprises a variety of styles and décors'.[4] The Courtaulds, who had no children to succeed them, left Eltham at the end of the Second World War and moved to Zimbabwe. For the remainder of the lease, Eltham was occupied by the Army Education Service, who treated the house with respect, and on their departure in 1995, English Heritage took over the property, remaking much of the original furniture in a spirit of make-believe that is entirely appropriate.

Seely and Paget never attached themselves to any single style. Partly because one of Paget's uncles was the Bishop of Chester, they

ELTHAM PALACE, LONDON Top: *The circular entrance hall, by the Swedish designer Rolf Engströmer, is top-lit with glass pavement lights, their shape matched by the Marion Dorn rug below.*

Above: *It was eccentric to imitate a French château while extending a medieval royal palace with interiors like those of an ocean liner.*

Left: *The lacquered doors of the dining room open on to a view of the entrance hall.*

TEMPLEWOOD, NORFOLK   Top: *Samuel Hoare, Lord Templewood,*
was an enthusiast for the villas of Andrea Palladio, and instructed his nephew Paul Paget
to build one for him.

Above: *Templewood sits at the crossing point of wide vistas through woodland.*

TEMPLEWOOD, NORFOLK Above: *The bedrooms at Templewood are ranged around the central saloon, with furniture and pictures from the Hoare and Gurney families. When Paul Paget inherited the house, he commissioned a Baroque ceiling from the painter Brian Thomas.*

specialised in churches, some of which were relatively modern in style. Their other country house of the 1930s was Templewood in Norfolk, built for another of Paget's uncles, Sir Samuel Hoare, the MP and Cabinet Minister under Stanley Baldwin. Unusually, the client himself wrote the article published in *Country Life* in February 1939, describing his desire for 'a small house on a big site', which he also referred to as a 'Petit Trianon'. The idea of compactness was growing in attraction during the twentieth century, both for the visual coherence it could provide and for the imagined ease and economy of management. The eighteenth century offered examples besides the Petit Trianon, most of them ultimately derived from the villas of Andrea Palladio, with which Sir Samuel was familiar. Most cultivated Englishmen would still have been prejudiced against Palladio, even by

the late 1930s, since earlier writers, including Hussey himself, had condemned his influence as foreign to the warmth and reasonableness that were seen as the prime attributes of Georgian domestic design.

At Templewood, however, it is not the true rigour of Palladio that is represented, but rather a stage version, employing materials salvaged from Nuthall Temple – a centrally planned Georgian villa near Nottingham demolished in 1929 – principally ironwork and a fine pair of sphinxes. Since the Nuthall columns were too tall, a set of Ionic columns was rescued from the rebuilding of the Bank of England in order to form a loggia and entrance portico, out of scale and out of style with the other details, giving a clear indication that accuracy was never the intention. In reality, Templewood is a rather grand bungalow raised up on a basement storey, with a double-height central hall, offering a very satisfactory scheme for modern weekend existence, described by Lady Cholmondley (Sir Philip Sassoon's sister) as 'little wagon-lit compartments round the edge'.[5] The service accommodation is fitted into the north wing, and does not interrupt the compact geometry of the plan.

A different approach to invoking the Palladian past is found at Charters in Sunningdale, Berkshire, a large house designed for Frank Parkinson, an inventor and manufacturer of electrical equipment, by the architects Adie Button and Partners, who were normally specialists in industrial buildings. In planning Charters, they managed with some success to recreate a vision of a grand country house in the language of the Modern Movement, and raised questions about the compatibility of these concepts. When Modernism viewed itself as dynamic and asymmetrical, it contradicted Classical principles, but Le Corbusier's formula of architecture as 'a skilful, exact and magnificent game of volumes assembled beneath the light' was applicable to the eighteenth-century ideal of the clear-cut solid of a pale-coloured house rising from a sea of green. Le Corbusier himself invoked the Classical calm of Palladio's villas in the design of his most famous building, the Villa Savoye at Poissy, France, in 1929, while K. F. Schinkel's villas for the Prussian royal family of the 1820s were always in the mind of Mies van der Rohe. Eighteenth-century precedent also sanctioned the idea of importing a more rigorous style into England from Continental Europe.

Externally, Charters resolves the contradictions with a double-height abstracted portico, of a kind found on many Italian public buildings of the Fascist period, and a mixture of horizontal and vertical fenestration, all providing incident in a single solid volume of white, stone-clad building. Perhaps the mathematical grid of 1 foot 10

CHARTERS, BERKSHIRE Above and left: *This grand country house is delicately poised between Modernism and the Classical tradition, recalling Italian public architecture of the 1930s. The house sits on a raised plinth in the midst of an eighteenth-century-style park landscape.*

inches used by the architects for their dimensions and reflected in the windowpanes and squares of the stone cladding helps to achieve unity. Internally, the Rococo taste of ironwork balustrades and of Martin Battersby's mural betrays a greater confusion, introduced by the decorator, Mrs G. R. Mount, to gratify the taste of Mrs Parkinson. Some of the simpler rooms, such as the morning room, with paintings by Adrian Daintry of modern life inset into the walls, seem the most successful, in the style described by Osbert Lancaster as 'Vogue Regency'. This was a variation on Art Deco whose restraint made it popular in Britain. There was very little ornament on the walls, cornices or fireplaces, and to that extent it was modern, but the rooms were usually arranged symmetrically around a fireplace, with lit recesses on either side to hold cut flowers. As with the smart clothes of the period, it was important that everything matched in colour and fabric. A horizontal cut-off at dado level governed furniture and fittings, so that the upper half of the room, painted in a uniform pale colour, was often blank apart from a few carefully chosen paintings. As Lancaster wrote, 'So long as no attempt is made to follow the fatal will-o'-the-wisp of period accuracy, Vogue Regency remains as suitable a style as any for a period in describing which the phrase Transitional, it is now apparent, is the grossest of understatements.'[6]

CHARTERS, BERKSHIRE Top: *The hall is overlooked by a gallery linking the main bedroom areas, with an accomplished Rococo balustrade.*

Above: *The morning room, with paintings by Adrian Daintry fixed to the walls.*

Left: *The inter-war taste for Italian Baroque was appropriate to the scale of the main hall, based on a colour scheme of cream, gold and terracotta. The mural, since painted over, was by Martin Battersby, who became an expert on the history of this period of decoration.*

If one was looking for the architectural as well as the decorative demonstration of Vogue Regency, no example would serve better than Gribloch, Stirlingshire, one of the few major Scottish houses of the 1930s. The architect, Basil Spence (1907–76), then based in Edinburgh, was thirty years old. Although he had spent some time working for Lutyens in London, he also experimented with Modernism with his partner, William Kininmonth. In 1936, Spence designed Broughton Place and Quothquhan, both in Lanarkshire and both accomplished reworkings of the Scottish Renaissance. John Colville, the client for Gribloch, who had inherited a fortune based on a Glasgow steelworks, was related to the client for Quothquhan. His American wife later brought in the New York architect Perry Duncan to speed up the job, as Spence was occupied with the Empire Exhibition in Glasgow, where Colville had helped him to secure the job of designing the Scottish pavilions.

Spence was skilled at bridging the gap between tradition and Modernism, as he demonstrated at Coventry Cathedral, which made his name in 1951 – the same year that *Country Life* published Gribloch. If Charters was a reworking of Palladian ideas, then the shallow curve of the entrance front at Gribloch, terminating in a balconied bow window, with smooth, white-painted surfaces, was directly inspired by the Regency. The biography of John Nash published in 1935 by John Summerson, who was briefly one of Spence's teachers at Edinburgh College of Art, signalled a revival of interest in the informal planning of the Regency. The bowed end of Gribloch's living room, with a first-floor balcony wrapping around it, combined with the smooth stucco finish and the Classical proportions of the windows, recreated the period effect.

The skilful interlocking of the oval and round-ended rooms on the plan, where the house is bent into a curve to make the best of the spectacular views, indicates that Spence might also have studied one of his Scots antecedents, Robert Adam. To the south, Spence planned a suntrap between splayed wings, with an outdoor swimming pool overlooked by the double-height windows. Internally, these windows run behind the elegantly curving staircase in an oval hall, the centre-piece of a decorative scheme by John Hill of Green and Abbott, leaders in Vogue Regency style, whom, in the words of Michael Hall in 1998, the Colvilles 'bombarded with pages torn from *House Beautiful* and other American interior design magazines'.

The cornice decoration was formed from shells and rope, with shell chairs and a carpet with shell motifs in pale blues, turquoise and mauve. As Michael Hall wrote, 'the swimming pool sends dancing reflections into the room on even the greyest day'.[7] After much consideration, including a consultation with the art historian Nikolaus Pevsner (who was then working for the furniture-makers Gordon Russell), the staircase was designed by Raymond Stubes of Paris. The wrought-iron stair balustrade, surmounted by an aluminium handrail,

GRIBLOCH, STIRLINGSHIRE *The curving entrance front commands a spectacular view towards the Grampians. The crisp white geometry of Basil Spence's design creates a self-contained volume in the Scottish castle tradition.*

was made in Edinburgh. The colour scheme of the drawing room included a pale-blue ceiling, plum carpet and oyster walls, with curtains hand-painted with a large-scale floral pattern in plum, lime green, pink and pale blue.

Gribloch was carefully equipped for the enjoyment of a traditional country-house lifestyle assisted by modern conveniences. In the extensive service wing, the kitchen was fully fitted, a rarity at this time, while a linen room and drying room, with special stretchers for long socks, were provided upstairs. Several key pieces of furniture were designed by Betty Joel, in a *moderne* style (a streamlined form of Art Deco). She was successful both as a designer and a business-woman, and the curving shapes that she liked to use perfectly complemented the architecture. These original pieces were cherished by the owners who succeeded the Colvilles in 1984, making a unique ensemble of its kind, so that when Gribloch was placed on the market in 1997, the National Trust for Scotland tried to acquire it, urged on by *Country Life*, but sadly without success.

After 1930, the idea of a 'middle way' between Modernism and tradition was often spoken about, but seldom in terms that presented

GRIBLOCH, STIRLINGSHIRE Above: *A guest bedroom.*
Below and right: *The staircase, decorated in sugary blues and mauves.*

anything other than a compromise. The pragmatism shown by architects such as Basil Spence at Gribloch in consulting the wishes of the client might be viewed with suspicion by advocates of either of the extreme positions. It is therefore interesting to find, in the country-house descriptions written by Christopher Hussey at intervals through the 1930s, the emergence of a deeper consideration of how the middle ground might be identified.

Birchens Spring in Beaconsfield, Buckinghamshire, by John Campbell (1878–1947), was completed in 1934 and covered by *Country Life* in 1938, when Hussey wrote: 'There is about its outward aspect a boldness, and yet a sensitiveness, and a feeling for the substance of the building, that calls to mind the best elements in our heritage of building craftsmanship.'[8] For most readers, Campbell was a new discovery, although he had become famous in Germany, where he practised before the First World War. One of his houses in the Berlin suburbs was even sketched by the young Le Corbusier. Rebuilding a career in England in the 1920s had been a painful and slow process for Campbell, and Birchens Springs was his first major new building, following his return from a second professional stint in Germany. While part of Campbell's attraction for the Germans was his Englishness, his work in England shows Central European

BIRCHENS SPRING, BUCKINGHAMSHIRE Top: *The entrance courtyard shows a play of shapes, enclosing a generous space. The arch to the left leads to a stableyard.*

Above: *Another view of the exterior; the composition of separate volumes offers many different pictures.*

Left: *The risers of the staircase are decorated with coloured marble.*

characteristics, but so subtly blended that no individual national style predominates. Such was Campbell's intention, as he believed that Modernism was the last in a sequence of false moves in architecture, including an over-concern with style as an independent issue, but that it was still possible to unpick the past and start again.

Birchens Spring is, therefore, in part at least, a direct response to modern architecture. It has the overall whiteness and the asymmetrical planning typical of Modernism, but, in a more traditional manner, it minimises window area, heightens the roofs and allows a role for fine craftsmanship. Thus, rather than diluting the extremes of opposing styles, Campbell took strengths from each of them, including a rigorous underlying geometric grid. One distinguishing factor of his designs is the principle of 'a roof for each room', meaning a reversal of the Renaissance innovation of the double-pile plan. The result adds light to the rooms, and produces the exciting overall geometry of masses at Birchens Spring, including the cylindrical tower that houses the dining room in the entrance courtyard. Internally, the house makes for interesting exploration with a particularly fine staircase. The square terrace garden enclosed within the two main ranges of the house adds to the pattern of ordered enclosure.

After the war, Hussey wrote about a group of three houses by Campbell at Chapel Point in Mevagissey, Cornwall. The first of these, Chapel Point House, was built by Campbell for his wife, his son and himself, after he had bought the whole beautiful promontory site in 1933, and he added two other houses for sale up to 1938, intending to go on to develop a small community on the peninsula. Hussey was even more enthusiastic about these smaller works than he was about Birchens Spring, since they seemed particularly relevant to post-war conditions.

CHAPEL POINT, CORNWALL *John Campbell developed three houses on this rocky coastal site at Mevagissey, one of them (above) as his own home. The Gate House (right) makes a formal entranceway into a projected village, with the two other completed houses beyond. Campbell supervised the construction to demonstrate how traditional techniques could still be economically viable in the 1930s.*

Chapel Point was intended to demonstrate that it need not be any more expensive to build a traditional-looking house out of local stone than it was to build a standard pre-war bungalow of the kind that so disfigured the Cornish coastline. Continuing his principle of 'a roof for every room', although on a much smaller scale than at Birchens Spring, Campbell even succeeded in intensifying the architectural effect of enclosure and security that he believed was psychologically necessary in a house.

Campbell had been constantly present on the site during construction, demonstrating old techniques that the builders had forgotten, such as swept valleys in the roof tiling, and making adjustments to the design in the light of experience. Local stone was used for the external walls and local earth formed into blocks for the inner ones, with Delabole slate for the floors. The results, still fortunately surviving in good condition, have caught the imagination of all those who have seen them, whether arriving by land or sailing past by sea. The interiors benefit from the reduced scale, especially Campbell's own house, its design based on a module of 9 feet that provides the width

CHAPEL POINT, CORNWALL Above left: *The living room of Gate House achieves grandeur with height. The ceiling beams were painted by Campbell himself.*

Above right: *The study in Campbell's own home, Chapel Point House, has a patterned brick fireplace. The arches beyond lead to the short flight of steps into the living room.*

Left: *The living room of Chapel Point House is a subtle asymmetric composition of space with a feeling of shelter.*

of the rooms. Hussey concluded his article by saying that if he were Duke of Cornwall, he would appoint Campbell his Minister of Works. The publication of the *Country Life* articles in 1945 created great interest and many inquiries, but owing to government priorities for reconstruction, private house building was almost impossible during the post-war period. Campbell, who died in a fall from the cliff near Chapel Point in 1947, was unable to reap the benefits of his new popularity.

Campbell admired the way that Arts and Crafts architects of the late nineteenth century had concentrated on the essence of home, while insisting on real materials and rescuing traditional building techniques from oblivion. During his time in Germany, he had a close-up view of the beginnings of Modernism, but while sympathetic to its aim of renewal, he felt that it was a mistake to see the history of architecture as a succession of styles with Modernism coming at the end to sweep all the others away.

In the last years of the war, the government expected that the manufacture of prefabricated houses would solve the housing problem, arguing that not enough men could be trained in traditional skills and that the use of brick, stone and timber would be too expensive. Campbell responded that the structure of a house 'is far too intimately associated with the ground upon which it lies, and the skies above it, ever to be suited to such a method'.[9] He felt that if the people of Britain were to value the country they had fought to protect, then such important things as new houses should demon-

strate the same sense of dignity and effort that had gone into the war. He believed that it was possible to provide the best quality for everyone, not only for the rich.

In both his articles, Hussey compared John Campbell to Edwin Lutyens, suggesting that, as a slightly younger man, Campbell had shared with Lutyens, Charles Rennie Mackintosh and the Swedish architect Ragnar Östberg a free and creative approach to tradition. In his account of Ridgemead, Surrey, the major country house designed by Sir Edwin's son Robert Lutyens (1901–72) in 1938, Hussey returned to the same theme of 'picking up the robust trend of architecture arrested by the last war'. It was a difficult job being the son of Britain's most famous architect, and Robert Lutyens began his career in the 1920s by concentrating on interior design. He collaborated with his father on Middleton Park, Sir Edwin's last substantial country house, and Ridgemead shows how he continued to learn from the same source, although Hussey noted 'a freshness and a sense of adventure that are the contribution of a younger man'. This was far from being a unique devotion, however, for many architects, including Oliver Hill and Francis Pollen among those represented in this book, owed much of their desire to design buildings to the inspiration of Lutyens' work.

The client for Ridgemead was Captain Woolf Barnato, a racing motorist, the son of the diamond millionaire Barney Barnato. He requested a house in Spanish Mission style, reflected in the emphasis of strength on the entrance front, but not otherwise over-intrusive. Like the later Edwin Lutyens houses, this side of the house is private and even slightly forbidding, leading through a series of veil-like transitional spaces before the living accommodation on the south side is reached. This also projects a series of advancing parallels, partially of enclosed space and partially imagined with what look like unfinished pergolas. None of Edwin Lutyens' houses achieved such a unification of inside and outside, and Robert wrote that he felt he could 'do a lot to resolve antagonisms between the worlds of yesterday and tomorrow'.[10]

RIDGEMEAD, SURREY Above: *The service yard entrance, enclosed by a circular wall, would be grand enough for most front doors.*

Right above: *The client, Woolf Barnato, requested a Spanish Mission style, which suited Robert Lutyens' preference for blank walls flanking the main entrance.*

Right below: *The main section of the long garden elevation plays complex games of screening within the vocabulary of Mediterranean Classicism, and is complemented by the formal terrace.*

The article on Ridgemead, published in 1940, included Hamstone House (see page 13) among those buildings 'picking up the robust trend'. Not many miles away at St George's Hill, this house for Peter Lind, the owner of a contracting firm, was designed by Forbes and Tate, a general-purpose practice with no particular stylistic convictions. The plan shows a strongly diagrammatic geometry, beginning with a forecourt struck from a circle. To this is applied, on the garden front, a splayed layer of two principal rooms on two storeys. A solarium rises above, and an air-raid shelter for fifty people is concealed beneath the dining room to one side; this was a feature also found at Eltham Palace and several other large houses of the time. The curves and blocky shapes, undoubtedly robust, refer to both Modernism and the newly re-evaluated work of Sir John Vanbrugh, while the small-paned windows and yellow-stone facings, after which the house is named, are more specific Georgian references, fused, as Hussey believed, in the architect's approach to the problem. As with most of the 'middle way' houses, the interiors were more conservative than the exteriors, including a fine Rococo-style stair balustrade.

It was relatively rare in the inter-war period for architects to design houses for their own occupation, compared to the frequency with which this happened after the Second World War. Buttersteep House,

BUTTERSTEEP HOUSE, BERKSHIRE   Above: *The blank wall of the projecting bedroom wing is ornamented with a stone relief by the sculptor William Aumonier.*

Below: *A dell of broom, azalea and cherries was planted to the north of the house as part of an elaborately planned garden.*

Left: *The architect, Francis Lorne, used brick to make a formal composition of masses out of the stair tower.*

Berkshire, by Francis Lorne (1889–1963) was a large house built by one of the partners in John Burnet, Tait and Lorne, a firm of Scottish origin that made one of the most painless transitions from traditional to modern design, being highly accomplished in both spheres. Before Lorne returned from a spell of work in the United States, Thomas Tait had designed the houses at Silver End, Essex, that were *Country Life*'s first offering of Modernism in 1928 (see pages 8–9). The assembly of masses at Buttersteep, best seen from the approach drive, is typical of the firm's work of the time, apparently derived largely from the example of the Dutch architect W. M. Dudok, who in turn was influenced by Frank Lloyd Wright. The use of yellow Dutch bricks would have emphasised the connection. Slightly conservative among modern houses for 1938, Buttersteep House was not published in *Country Life* until 1942.

Set in a similar landscape of acid soil in the south-western Home Counties, The Homewood in Esher, Surrey, built in 1938 by Patrick Gwynne (1913–2003), was architecturally representative of a more radical strain of Modernism. The commission arose because the Gwynne family already owned a house next to the Portsmouth Road. Increasing traffic during the 1930s made it undesirable, but the garden was large enough to allow for a new house much further away

THE HOMEWOOD, SURREY Above: *The bedroom wing, by Patrick Gwynne, is the first element to meet the eye of the approaching visitor, who drives beneath it to reach the front door.*

Right: *The dining room opens on to the upper deck, with space beneath for outdoor entertaining.*

Below: *The house is divided into two main volumes, with the principal rooms raised on brick piers to command a view of the garden.*

from the noise. Commander Gwynne commissioned the house from his son, who had seen High and Over while on a sketching expedition from Harrow School and been immediately attracted to Modernism. The design of The Homewood grew largely from the conditions of the brief and the site. In order to get the best views over the garden, it was desirable to place the main living accommodation on the first-floor level. This was standard practice in the villas of Le Corbusier, which were already canonic works around the world. Instead of creating a single cubic mass of concrete on slender *piloti*, as an architect might have done earlier in the 1930s, Gwynne placed brick piers under the elevated box, forming a more English effect on the garden terrace. He broke the volume of the house up, separating the bedrooms into a wing like the cross bar of a T, linked at the point where the spiral stair ascends from the entrance, itself formed with a porte-cochère beneath the guest rooms.

The Homewood was designed with entertaining in mind, and the main open-plan living room is one of the most effective of its time, complete with a dance floor, a sound system and variable lighting. 'We danced like mad,' Gwynne recalled. When not cleared for dancing, the furniture was carefully positioned to create different sitting areas for daytime and evening use. The dining room forms a bay at the corner of the house, with its own external terrace and stair down to a small swimming pool.

THE HOMEWOOD, SURREY Above: *The dining-room terrace demonstrates the Modernist principle of space flowing between indoors and outdoors.*

Right: *The main living room offers open-plan living on a grand scale, furnished over time with pieces designed or selected by the architect-owner, Patrick Gwynne.*

Commander Gwynne referred to The Homewood as 'the temple of costly experience', but it started the young Patrick on a career primarily devoted to house design, continuing into the 1970s.[11] He moved into The Homewood and ran his architectural practice from the house. In 1992, he offered the house to the National Trust, making it the second major Modern Movement house to be thus preserved and made available to the public, with the unusual distinction that the original architect was able to spend ten years working on its restoration, and on clearing some of the growth in the garden to restore the original sight lines.

The Homewood and No. 2 Willow Road, Hampstead, by Ernö Goldfinger (1902–87) are the only examples of Modernist houses from the period to have survived in continuous occupation with an accumulation of furniture and decoration, a compelling argument in each case for their protection by the National Trust. Goldfinger had moved from his native Hungary to study architecture in Paris during the most exciting years of the 1920s. He was friendly with many artists, including some of the leading Surrealists, and his English wife, Ursula, became a pupil with Amédée Ozenfant, one of the founders of the Purist movement, on his recommendation. Works by Ozenfant, Henry Moore and later British artists hang in the house, while

NO. 2 WILLOW ROAD, LONDON Above: *The back of the terrace of three houses; the balcony opens off the living room of No. 2, Ernö Goldfinger's house.*

Left: *The first floor combines three rooms with folding doors. The living room at the back of the house connects with the studio beyond, with a drop in floor level. The dining room is out of sight to the left.*

Below: *A giant frame in the living room provides space for small pictures.*

PERFECTLY MODEST

1950-60

In 1949, the *Country Life* writer R. Randal Phillips, introducing the third edition of his book *Houses for Moderate Means*, warned his readers that 'a house which was built for, say, £1,200 in 1937 would cost £3,000 today – assuming that a licence for it were granted and that materials were available'.[1] Private building was virtually illegal even for men of great means until 1954, but from that date onwards, new houses began to appear with increasing frequency.

In post-war Britain, good design was one of the services that the Welfare State sought to provide indirectly through exhibitions and publications. Design professionals worried about the poor quality of public taste and hoped that the simplicity of modern design would appeal to a younger generation flocking to the Festival of Britain in 1951, and moving into homes in the new towns.

NO. 20 BLACKHEATH PARK, LONDON Above: *Peter Moro's house emphasises the contrast of wall and window.*

NO. 6 BACONS LANE, LONDON Left: *Leonard Manasseh's house in Highgate reveals its inner structure, while* Sarah, *a sculpture from the 1951 Festival of Britain, stands watch.*

NO. 20 BLACKHEATH PARK, LONDON *Above: The living space, photographed in 2000, before the dispersal of Peter Moro's furnishings and the abstract constructions by him on the wall.*

Left: The staircase is treated as an extension of the living space, and a diagonal vista extends to the dining room. The photograph was taken in 1958.

Peter Moro (1911–98), a pre-war German émigré, was the designer of the interiors of the Royal Festival Hall. Like many architects of the 1950s, he worked mainly in the public sector, but his principal post-war house design, No. 20 Blackheath Park, was built in 1957 for himself and his family. The house is a compact rectangle, with a timber-clad upper floor projecting over the brick walls below, containing the main living room. This arrangement was found in many American houses of the 1940s designed by architects such as Marcel Breuer, and became popular in Britain ten years on, since there had been few British opportunities to experiment in the years between. This scheme was economical in construction, and less 'boxy' than the cubic flat-roofed modern houses of the 1930s. Like the Festival Hall, it tries to give an effect of weightlessness.

Internally, the space was planned with minimum partitioning between rooms, although there is a split level running through the long axis, making interesting vistas between the kitchen, living room and study areas. This was typical of the post-war style of living without servants. As H. Dalton Clifford explained when Blackheath Park was published in *Country Life*, 'Privacy is comparatively unimportant in a servantless family house – the children can always be packed off to their bed-sitting rooms to do their homework for with modern methods of heating, one can be sure that every part of every room will be comfortably warm. But it is of great importance that the lady of the house should be able to cook while supervising the children's games, entertaining guests, telling her husband the latest local gossip, listening to the wireless, watching television or generally playing her proper role in the family scene.'[2]

This passage shows how the impact of central heating and living without servants was still something to be remarked upon. The effect of these developments on house planning was liberating, for the need to create privacy and to conserve heat in earlier houses had restricted the theoretical idea of open planning that modern architects wished to put into practice. While it was relatively easy to design an open-plan room in a large house, such as The Homewood, Surrey (see pages 78–81), smaller houses called for greater ingenuity from the architect to ensure that everything worked from an aesthetic as well

as a practical point of view. Continuous boarded ceiling surfaces help to unify the spaces at Blackheath Park, while the use of a sliding door between the stair landing and the living room increases the potential for long-distance views in what is still not a particularly large house.

Michael Ventris (1922–56) was another architect building his own house in the 1950s, in Hampstead, the North London equivalent of Blackheath to the south. At the time of his tragic early death at the age of thirty-four, Ventris had made significant steps towards deciphering the ancient Minoan script Linear B, an occupation that, while secondary to his work as an architect, has ensured his fame, and was achieved in large part because he applied the same techniques of analysis and teamwork to the script that he was using to develop new methods for school construction. No. 19 North End was his one completed building, designed in conjunction with his wife, Lois. Its extreme compactness and simplicity show the effect of building restrictions still in force in 1953, and the shallow pitched roof (a concession to common sense) was not considered to exclude a house from being thought 'modern' at this time.

Like the Moro house, it places the living room on the first floor, with the ground floor operating, at least in daytime, primarily as a children's realm. No longer did nannies supervise children in a remote nursery, but, as Mark Girouard wrote in 1959, 'the parents and children can be noisy or quiet according to their needs'.[3] This was the beginning of the sharing of space between adults and children that is now normal for many households. The mother was now not only the cook, but also the chief childminder, and it was important that the kitchen should offer surveillance of both indoor and outdoor play areas. It is interesting that, despite the advent of central heating,

NO. 19 NORTH END, LONDON Above: *Modern architects after the war admitted the practicality of traditional forms like the pitched roof and materials such as brick and timber.*

Left: *The living room and study (the other side of the fireplace) fill one end of the small house. The plywood furniture was designed by Marcel Breuer.*

most modern houses of the 1950s retained a fireplace, although this
would often, as in the Ventris house, stand in the middle of a room
rather than being placed against a wall.

One remarkable feature of the house was the number of furnishings
by Marcel Breuer, who, during two years of residence in London in
the later 1930s, designed the interiors of the Highgate flat where
Ventris lived with his mother. These included built-in pieces around
which the dimensions of the new house were organised in a remarkable act of homage. The large plywood armchairs with spaces for
books seemed dated in 1959, but nonetheless sold for large sums
when they were finally removed from the house in 2002 and were
acquired by the Victoria and Albert Museum.

Across the lane from the Ventris house, Kenneth Capon (1915–
88), another architect, built a similar small house in 1951. He was a
member of Architects' Co-Partnership, a firm that made its name just
after the war with the Brynmawr rubber factory in Wales. Most of the
partners built themselves small houses in Hampstead or Highgate
during the 1950s, and Capon also built a holiday house at Bosham
Hoe near Chichester, West Sussex, which was often illustrated as it
showed how even a cheap house could have a quality of delight and
fantasy.

UPPER WOLVES COPSE, SUSSEX Top: *Kenneth Capon's house is
raised among the trees on a slender concrete frame.*

Above: *The dining area overlooks the large outdoor deck. The kitchen is
fully integrated into the main living space.*

Left: *Victorian table and chairs find their place comfortably in the modern
surroundings.*

While we have seen that upper-storey living was popular in the 1950s, Upper Wolves Copse, completed in 1955, had virtually no ground storey. The house was raised up 7 feet on narrow concrete posts, and an open stair ascended to a wide platform outside the front door, with the woodland undergrowth coming up to it almost uninterrupted. The pitched roof has deep eaves, protecting the large windows, for the absence of any neighbours, combined with the screen of trees, meant that there were none of the usual concerns about privacy. The compactness of the planning reminded Mark Girouard of 'a kind of woodland yacht sailing in air instead of water'. Although it is now the annexe to a much larger and more solid house designed for later owners by Michael Grice, another partner of Architects' Co-Partnership following Capon's death, Upper Wolves survives almost unaltered.

The fourth in this sequence of architects' own houses, No. 6 Bacons Lane in Highgate, London, built in 1959 by Leonard Manasseh (born 1916), stands in a cul-de-sac of houses of similar period, two of which were built by partners of Architects' Co-Partnership. Manasseh was only slightly younger than these young turks of the Architectural Association School, and launched his career with some small buildings in the Festival of Britain. The sculpture in

his garden, *Sarah* by Daphne Hardy Henrion, was made to stand at the base of the '51 Bar, which he designed for the South Bank exhibition to conceal a block of lavatories.

Manasseh's house enjoys southward views over Highgate Cemetery towards London, so it was natural to put the major living rooms upstairs. Like the Ventris house, his design places children's bedrooms along with kitchen and dining room on the ground floor, with easy access to the garden. The entry is at a mid-level, so that visitors can be directed either way. The steeply pitched roof allows for a third storey, with a painting studio in the form of a gallery over the living room. This solution was necessary as a legal covenant on the site limited the building to two floors.

An unusual feature of this house is the use of salvaged materials, from the old yellow London stock bricks of the external walls to Victorian printed and glazed tiles, and the tops of marble washstands sliced up to make the floors of the main living room, with electric

---

NO. 6 BACONS LANE, LONDON Right: *By opening up the roof space, Leonard Manasseh made a studio overlooking the living room.*

Below: *The main living room softens its raw brick walls with pictures, plants and a marble floor with underfloor heating.*

underfloor heating. The indoor plants are also worthy of remark, since these were a popular feature in modern houses in the 1950s in a way that they never had been in pre-war Modernism, when a few cacti were as much as one could expect. The fashion originated in Sweden and Denmark and was felt to soften the undecorated surfaces of Modernism. At No. 6 Bacons Lane, however, there are competing attractions in the form of bookshelves and a closely hung collection of contemporary paintings.

If one common feature of the houses considered in this chapter so far is that each is basically a box, then other houses can be found from the same period that take the opportunity to vary the box shape in different ways. The advantage of the box is that the small 'footprint' of the house saves on the cost of foundations, while in an urban setting, the least amount of garden is lost under the building. A compact roof is also the easiest kind to build and maintain. At other times, however, the potential of a site calls for a more varied solution. This was the case with the house at Toys Hill, Kent, designed by Philip Powell (1921–2002) and Hidalgo Moya (1920–94) in 1955. These architects had designed the Skylon, the 'vertical feature' on the South Bank, in 1951, while also constructing the large Churchill Gardens housing estate in Pimlico. Small houses were at the opposite

end of the scale, but Toys Hill was individually tailored to the site and the clients. Unusually, this was not a family house in the conventional sense, but built for two sisters, Monica and Muriel Anthony, who both had jobs in London and wanted a weekend retreat.

The plan of the house separates the main living rooms from the bedrooms in 'pavilions' with the hallway between them. The rooms are arranged to get the best views to the south and east over the Weald of Kent, shaded by overhanging edges of the flat roofs. The character of the house is relieved from being a conventional bungalow by the addition of a box room with an angled roof, which is really an extension of the garage, placed higher than the front door because of the slope of the drive. The ability to devise solutions for these rather unconventional kinds of site was a distinguishing feature of modern architecture both at this time and later. Inside, the house is notable for the provision of shelves at various heights for the display of ornamental objects. Some of these evidently included inherited possessions, as did the furnishings in the house, and it was typical of modern interiors of this time to mix old and new. Indeed, it was part

TOYS HILL, KENT Above: *A rare domestic work by Powell and Moya, one of the leading post-war architectural practices.*

of the policy of *House & Garden* magazine to encourage its readers to collect antiques suitable for display in modern interiors.

Horizontality has been identified as a typical characteristic of modern architecture. Frank Lloyd Wright developed the overhanging eaves and shallow roof pitches of his early houses in response to the flat prairie landscape around Chicago in the early years of the twentieth century, and long, low lines were adopted by European Modernists over the next thirty years. Although there were relatively few direct imitators of Wright in Britain, many post-war houses were designed as single-storey buildings under a single roof. The Walled Garden in Hurley, Berkshire, designed in 1956 by the architect Walter Goddard, is a good example. The site, part of a larger estate broken up into building plots, was typical for a modern house of the time, and Goddard wished to avoid overtopping the existing 10-foot-high garden walls. The projecting eaves along the garden front extend unbroken to embrace an outdoor terrace. Inside, the lengthways boarding of the ceiling again emphasises the horizontal and enlarges the scale, sympathetically echoed in the Regency stripes of some of the upholstery.

At Farnley Hey, near Huddersfield, 1954, by the architect Peter Womersley (1923–93), a different form of Frank Lloyd Wright's

THE WALLED GARDEN, BERKSHIRE Top: *The simple box form was intelligently adapted to its site by Walter Goddard.*

Above: *The open-plan interior with antique furniture.*

FARNLEY HEY

influence is apparent in the deliberate contrast between materials. While 1930s Modernism was mostly based on the idea of a dominant single material, whether concrete, brick or timber, there was a reaction in the 1950s in favour of an effect more like a Cubist collage, in which different surfaces and planes were made distinctive by the different materials in which they were faced. In this way, architects overcame the loss of ornament and pattern in Modernism, believing that the natural grain and pattern of timber or marble offered an appropriate substitute. Natural and manufactured materials were set off against each other. For example, the end wall of Farnley Hey is built of sandlime bricks – a smooth, pale-coloured material that was really a form of concrete and was both cheaper and more readily available than conventional fired bricks in the post-war years. This contrasts with other walls of rough local limestone, salvaged from a railway siding. Large sheets of glass are juxtaposed with oiled and varnished vertical shiplap timber boarding on the upper parts of the house. A narrow band of lemon-yellow Formica under the kitchen window lifts the side elevation with a typical 1950s colour, while the bold lettering of the house name is used as another piece of decoration.

Like the foyers of the Royal Festival Hall, Farnley Hey is designed to create a feeling of openness, with large windows overlooking a spectacular view where the ground falls sharply in front of the terrace. As at the Festival Hall, the space is not just a single box. The *Architectural Review* wrote at the time: 'The living room is differentiated into six main sub-divisions by changes in floor and ceiling level, and by visual hazards – the service core, staircase, sideboard and radiogram units, and the structural columns.'[4] The ladder stair rising from the hall to the gallery, and the vertical trellis behind it, maintain the feeling of open vistas.

This concentration on a single large room invites comparison with the hall of a medieval house, for one of the surprising outcomes of the introduction of central heating and the loss of servants was to make possible the return to a single shared living space. As the *Architectural Review* explained, 'the whole area can be opened up for large parties, or the different parts of it used separately and isolated for smaller gatherings, largely by changes in artificial lighting'.

The double-height space helps to make the structure of the house visible, as one would find in a timber-framed vernacular building. In this respect, Farnley Hey was a continuation of Chermayeff's use of a prominent structural frame at Bentley Wood, but Womersley's version is more varied in its use of materials and more dynamic in the composition of the different elements, such as the oversailing balcony cantilevered from a rubble stone wall at the corner between the entrance side and the terrace overlooking the main view.

The broad gallery overlooking the hall was intended as a place where musicians could perform at parties, and the high room with its

FARNLEY HEY, YORKSHIRE *One of the earliest of the larger Post-Modernist houses, sited on the brow of a steep hill. The projection at the left-hand end was originally an open balcony, closed off with a timber face.*

wooden ceiling created excellent acoustics both for live and recorded sound that could be 'tuned' by drawing the big curtain across the window. One peculiarity of the 1950s was that ordinary softwood was often more difficult to obtain than more exotic hardwoods, because the available stocks had been felled for use during the war and it took time for new supplies to grow. At Farnley Hey the floor of the big room is made of camphorwood, with a surround of salvaged York stone flags.

The dining room is reached down a few steps, offering a worm's-eye view of the living room from its lower level across a plant trough; since the end of the 1930s, British architects had learnt from Continental examples how to make provision for growing plants and would even specify particular plants for different parts of their buildings, thus contributing to the ideal of unifying indoors and outdoors.

Fortunately, Farnley Hey has survived well in the hands of the present owners, who bought it from the Womersleys in 1958. As one of the earliest of the larger post-war Modernist houses, it was widely illustrated and epitomised the changes in modern domestic architecture after the war. Unlike many of his contemporaries, Peter Womersley made a specialism of individual house design, and built two more houses for his brother, the original client for Farnley Hey, as he moved from one part of the country to another.

Womersley based his practice in Scotland, where many of his best surviving buildings are to be found. For the textile designer Bernat Klein, he designed a house and studio as separate buildings near Selkirk in the Scottish Borders; the house, High Sunderland, completed in 1957, was one of the most striking among the mixed bunch of new houses illustrated in *Country Life* in the second half of the decade. It shares with Farnley Hey an evident interest in the display of structure and geometry, but instead of the Picturesque variety of the earlier house, it is as tightly controlled as a Palladian villa, sitting lightly as a clear rectangle outlined in white-painted timber on its hilltop sea of green grass.

As Mark Girouard explained in 1960, the design is based on a module of 8 feet, which is subdivided in regular units to create glazing

FARNLEY HEY, YORKSHIRE   Right: *Despite the addition of radiators in the gallery (intended to accommodate musicians at parties), the open spaces are retained as originally designed.*

Below: *Although it was not an expensive house, fine timber and stone were used to create richness in the double-height living room.*

divisions. The overall rectangle consists of a mixture of solid and void, as in some places the windows and walls come at the outer edge, while more often they are set back to create terraces and court-yards. These were the sort of formal games promoted in art schools of the 1950s as the grammar of modern design, applicable equally to painting, sculpture and architecture. Womersley turned the Mediterranean reciprocity of indoor and outdoor space into a sophis-ticated piece of design, which was enhanced by the colours of exotic hardwoods – idigbo, maple, rosewood and walnut – and the curtains and fabrics produced at Bernat Klein's own mill.

Although High Sunderland is only one storey, it uses small changes of level with a sunken seating area in the living room, a device that was becoming popular in American houses at this time. The plan provides a room for a resident housekeeper, so that although the kitchen is placed at a pivotal point between the adult and child zones of the house, it does not open up towards the entertaining areas.

The interplay of indoor and outdoor space is one of the planning principles found at No. 16 Kevock Road, Lasswade, 1960, a house near Edinburgh by the architects James Morris (born 1931) and Robert Steedman (born 1929), who were responsible for an exciting

HIGH SUNDERLAND, BORDERS Top and above: *The rectangle of the house, defined by a white-painted architrave, is partly filled in and partly opened out to create courtyards and terraces.*

Left: *The main living room is 50 feet long. The fireplace in the foreground serves a smaller sitting area overlooking the main part of the room.*

series of house designs during the 1960s when modern architecture in Scotland was creating its own distinct culture.

The site was 'on top of a precipitous slope' as Mark Girouard wrote in 1960, 'looking down a deep and bold valley to the distant chimneys of a paper-mill, placed as dramatically as any Georgian landscape architect could desire'.[5] With only 15 feet of level ground between the access road running along the rear and a steep drop into a valley below, previously nobody had thought it would be possible to build here, but Morris and Steedman rose to the challenge for their client, Ian Wilson, a printer.

The house was partly cantilevered out over the slope, with a solid brick structure rising direct from the edge of the road and lightweight materials supported on steel making a contrasting type of architecture facing the view on the other side. This is a demonstration of the versatility of modern architecture as an experimental way of combining structure and materials without any preconceptions about the final appearance. The plan takes the form of an extended pavilion, at one end of which an open terrace, paved with lithographic printing stones, is formed between the living room and the oblique wall of the garage. This outdoor room is suggestive of some of the famous Case Study Houses in and around Los Angeles sponsored by *Arts and*

Architecture magazine in the 1950s, and widely publicised at the time and in more recent years. Several of them use similar hilltop sites, the most famous of which was the house at Santa Monica built for themselves by the designers, Charles and Ray Eames in 1945–49. Other examples, like House No. 22, designed by Pierre Koenig in 1959–60, jut out dramatically with steel structures over precipices to obtain their spectacular views.

NO. 16 KEVOCK ROAD, LASSWADE, MIDLOTHIAN
Above: *The house by Morris and Steedman is designed to cope with a narrow plot on the edge of a hill. The living room shows how the house is a series of parallel layers.*

Right: *Heavy structure to the rear supports a lighter layer, forming a glazed gallery linking the main rooms.*

There is a way through between the sheltering walls of No. 16 Kevock Road, so that after visitors have left their cars by the garage, they can come straight on to the terrace rather than through the house via the front door. Once you reach the terrace, the open angle of the walls makes a suntrap, with the overhanging garage roof pierced with openings so that patches of sunlight fall on to the wall below. Looking the other way, the cross section of the house is dramatically revealed, with its line of windows linking up the living room, dining room, kitchen and main bedroom. Although there are doors to close off the bedroom and kitchen, these are all in line with each other like a French enfilade, so that it is possible to see all the way from one end of the long narrow house to the other.

Another continuous passageway runs along the windowless back wall of the house, so that, as one looks at the plan, there is a central service 'core' containing the bathroom and kitchen, with passageways all round it. The bathroom has two doors, one from the master bedroom and another near the foot of the light wooden stair, suspended on steel, that rises to a small upper level containing two children's bedrooms. The placing of the bedrooms meant that it was effectively a single-storey house, with upstairs bedrooms that could be used as required. An unusual detail is the curved wall, interrupting the view in the rear passage, which marks the rounded end of the bathtub on its other side.

The drawing room has a fireplace set into a stone chimney-stack, with a screen wall connected to it, the result being somewhere between an inglenook and a theatrical stage, with a piece of uncut stone on the hearth to relieve the geometry – the sort of focal point that was often used by the architects of the Case Study Houses, in the spirit of Frank Lloyd Wright's use of natural boulders at Fallingwater, his most famous house of the 1930s. The wall does not rise all the way up to the ceiling but leaves a gap, which carries the view on into the dining room.

Mark Girouard compared the house to a ship in the way that it rides the hilltop, with its broad expanse of windows commanding the view rather like a ship's bridge. He went on to comment, 'As in much architecture of good quality, there is more than a reminiscence of naval architecture in this house; the architects seem to have been aiming, not at dignity or the Picturesque, but at some land-bound equivalent of the spare elegance, functional design and clean lines and colouring of a good yacht. This house admirably achieves, with its compact and sensible planning, its crisp contrast between dark wood and white walls and the trimness of its detailing.'[6]

Separation of parents and children has already been noted as a modification of the principle of open planning in family houses in the 1950s. At No. 3 Clarkson Road, Cambridge, designed by Trevor Dannatt for Peter Laslett in 1957, this became one of the leading motifs of the design. Situated on what was then the western edge of

NO. 16 KEVOCK ROAD, LASSWADE, MIDLOTHIAN *The upper storey, containing children's bedrooms, adds to the impressiveness of the house when seen from below.*

the city, amid a mixture of pre-war Neo-Georgian and Tudor, with the occasional modern white box of the 1930s, the Laslett house stands back from the road and originally looked over open fields. Trevor Dannatt (born 1920) was a young member of Peter Moro's design team for the Royal Festival Hall, and his contact with Peter Laslett, a young don at Trinity College, came about through a series of mutual friends. In its overall conception, the Clarkson Road house has common features with Moro's house in Blackheath Park, particularly in the placing of a timber box on top of a brick one. In this case, the main living room is positioned at the end of the upper box, rather than in the centre, and has a floor slightly lower than the other upstairs rooms, made possible by having the garage beneath it. The neat three-dimensional jigsaw of volumes was inspired by the same idea of *Raumplan*, emanating from Adolf Loos's Viennese practice earlier in the century, that can also be seen in Ernö Goldfinger's Willow Road houses.

Peter Laslett's academic research was concerned with the historical study of the 'nuclear family'. He wanted to build a modern house partly to discover how the needs of family could be reinterpreted, and

NO. 3 CLARKSON ROAD, CAMBRIDGE Top and above: *The Laslett house is an essay in the abstract composition of volumes and surfaces.*

Right: *The living room on the first floor is a spacious timber-lined cabin, higher than the other rooms.*

partly, in a missionary sense, to reintroduce a conservatively minded university town to the possibilities of modern architecture. The relationship between parents and children was part of the exploration. The solution is not a dramatic one, for it involves the designation of three zones: one for children on the ground floor next to the kitchen; another shared zone in the ground-floor dining room at the centre of the house; and the third, an adult zone, in the living room, which has a diagonal view through a glazed partition down the open stairs into the dining area, ensuring a degree of acoustic separation without isolation. The extra height in the living room, the unusual placing of the windows, and the sculptural quality of the brick chimney-stack all contribute to making this an open but secure-feeling space. The level of detail and control is retained throughout the house, which the

The pages of *Country Life* reveal that attempts in the 1930s to strike a balance between Modernism and tradition did not necessarily polarise into two extreme positions after the war. The manner of spanning this gap did change, however, and a house such as Serenity by Leslie Gooday (born 1921), at St George's Hill in Weybridge, Surrey, represents the work of an architect who enjoyed playing with architectural form rather more than some purist critics would have considered allowable. The roof-line falls towards the centre of the house in an unequal V or butterfly shape, a form originated by Le Corbusier in a project of 1930 and adopted by Marcel Breuer, among others, in the 1940s. At Serenity, the bedrooms are tucked under the fat end of the wedge, with a dramatic staircase leading to them like a bridge in the living room, which has a dining area on a higher level at

client treasured and proudly displayed up to his death in 2001. Colours were chosen by the architect for each of the four bedrooms compactly inserted into the upper floor, with a strong red for the downstairs playroom.

Like many architects who qualified during and just after the Second World War, Trevor Dannatt took delight in Nordic architecture. The house of the Finnish architect Alvar Aalto outside Helsinki was one inspiration for the timber-clad upper storey, while in Sweden Dannatt discovered the multi-cavity concrete blocks used in the solid walls of the lower part of the house. The house demonstrates the balance between technical thinking about economy of space and materials, and a sensitivity to the feeling of domestic space. The garden, linking the house to the road with borders of lavender and then opening more informally to the lawn behind, is a further demonstration of the careful thinking and aftercare that has been applied to this house.

There might be a way of classifying 1950s houses in relation to the prominence of their right angles. All those so far considered in this chapter would score highly, even when the roof is set at a different pitch. These include some by distinguished architects of the period, while the group of three houses that follows are by less well-known names, but take more interesting risks with design.

the other end. The play of space is simple and satisfactory, and, unlike the Moro and Laslett houses that have similar interior effects, it can find external expression.

The idea of making a big space in a small house was part of the thinking behind the Studio at Hemingford Grey, Huntingdonshire, built for the painter Elisabeth Vellacott by the architect Peter Boston (1918–99) in 1959. Mr Boston's mother was an old friend of Miss Vellacott, and they had shared the Manor at Hemingford Grey, a Norman stone house that was the basis for Mrs Boston's *Green Knowe* books. Typically for houses of its period, the Manor has a few large rooms, the main upper room of the house rising up to the roof with a broad stone chimney beside which a stair ascends. One cannot fail to see the affinity in the Studio, although here the main material is timber, with a brick chimney-stack.

Since money was limited, Mr Boston proposed an A-frame house, in which the roof comes right down to the ground and external walls are limited to the infilling of the gable ends. One end of the house rose to the full height, providing a tall window to light the painter's work and reveal the world beyond, while the other end of the house had a floor inserted, providing a compact kitchen and bathroom below and a single bedroom above, in the traditional studio form of a

platform overlooking the workspace. The elements are simple, but the way in which the staircase is taken up past the chimney is ingenious, while the diagonal lines of the roof are continued in the tongue-and-groove boarding, which also provides a honey-coloured warmth. Mr Boston tried on several subsequent occasions to obtain planning permission for houses of the same shape, believing them to be practical and beautiful, but they were always refused as being too unconventional.

The houses considered in this chapter so far have been modern, in the conventionally accepted sense that they do not make any deliberate reference to the past, but there has never been a period since 1930 when there has not been a mixture of co-existing styles. In the post-war period, it was assumed by many architects that to build in a traditional style would be too expensive, even if the materials and craftsmanship could be obtained. This was, however, demonstrably untrue. Sir Albert Richardson (1880–1964) had adopted a late-Georgian style for his domestic work before the First World War, when this actually represented a form of modernity, and his preferences did not change much thereafter.

Weston Patrick House, near Basingstoke in Hampshire, which Richardson designed in 1956, was commissioned after the client saw a new house of his in Bedford, published in *Country Life* with a text emphasising how elegance, if not extravagance, was still possible in the financially straitened post-war world. Weston Patrick is designed with such confident knowledge of the original sources that it could pass as a Georgian original to an uninformed eye, although the plan and the services allow for a more modern style of living.

After Great House, Dedham (see pages 94–5), executed in the late 1930s, Raymond Erith could have continued a career of designing houses not unlike Weston Patrick, but chose instead to make each of his commissions an opportunity for research and experiment. He believed that Classical architecture should develop in new directions, contradicting the assumption that it could only be nostalgic, while also going beyond the safe good taste adhered to by most of his clients. Erith generally worked backwards through time, examining the relationship between the architecture of Ancient Rome, the Italian Renaissance and its English derivatives.

SERENITY, SURREY Above: *Leslie Gooday varies the box-like shape typical of the 1950s house with a 'butterfly' roof, a popular form of the period.*

Right: *Airy staircases, varied light fittings and classic 1950s furniture create 'an astonishing sense of space'.*

As Mark Girouard succinctly wrote in his appraisal of Erith's Provost's Lodgings at Queen's College, Oxford, in 1960, 'Neo-Georgian architecture to-day is often so flabby or inept as to prove an embarrassment to its supporters; but here is a building that seems to show there is life in the old dog yet.'[7] Although the article ends by questioning whether Classicism can be more than a cul-de-sac, it raises issues of architectural context that are much better understood today than they were in 1960. The site was in the midst of one of the greatest congregations of Classical stone buildings in England, facing the Baroque library of Queen's College, and close to Hawksmoor's All Souls and Gibbs's Radcliffe Camera. Few of his contemporaries could have made a convincing addition within the same language, but Erith arguably succeeded, even if the elaborate rustication on his entrance front seems miniature in scale and lacking the three-dimensional projection found in eighteenth-century examples.

The architect's lengthy written account of the rationale of the house, published in Lucy Archer's monograph on Erith (1985), is well worth reading for the insight it gives into the practical as well as the symbolic and stylistic thinking contained in the design. Comparing the Provost's Lodgings to the equivalent buildings of All Souls and Lincoln College, Erith wrote, 'I have taken care that there will not be too much "architecture" ... and that what there is will not be too "good" – an important point, this.'[8]

Stephen Dykes Bower (1903–94) was an architect of the same generation as Raymond Erith and, like him, someone whose desire to continue architectural tradition made him feel increasingly isolated in the post-war years. Both men achieved much, but many opportunities were denied them because of the swing of official taste against their work. Dykes Bower concentrated on church work, and while particularly fond of Gothic design, he could also work effectively in the Classical style, as his great Baroque baldacchino in St Paul's Cathedral demonstrates.

St Vedast, Foster Lane, a little to the north of the cathedral, is a Wren church damaged by bombs and restored by Dykes Bower. The rebuilding offered the opportunity to provide a rectory beside the church where none had existed before, and Dykes Bower was called on to provide one of his few domestic designs. As with Erith's Provost's Lodgings, the two main façades of the house are contrasted in character. The street side shows a lot of plain brick, with a rusti-cated ground floor and four shallow arched recesses above, outlined with stone pilasters. The rhythm of four is succeeded by three on the floor above, and the frontage is completed with the stone outline of a pediment. The late Neo-Classical detail makes no attempt to imitate Wren, but like Erith's work at Oxford, this is a response in the same language.

THE STUDIO, HEMINGFORD GREY, HUNTINGDONSHIRE
Left: *Double-height space returns to its original use in an artist's studio house designed by Peter Boston.*

Right above: *The stairs to the bedroom wrap around the brick chimney-stack.*

Right below: *The shingled roof of the A-frame comes almost to the ground.*

The main outlook is to the courtyard at the rear, where a seventeenth-century brick building forms the parish hall, linked by a covered way to the street. The Rectory takes on a more London Regency character here, with four wide windows connected by an iron balcony. The ground level is raised on columns over a small cloister, while the top floor is divided between a study and a roof terrace. With a version of *piloti* holding it up, and a roof garden, the Rectory answers two of Le Corbusier's *Five Points of a New Architecture*, which he formulated in 1926, and shows how traditional style could be flexible and adaptable.

If Classical architects were frustrated by opposition in the 1950s, they were still in demand for the small number of country-house commissions that were given. For owners of existing country houses, the least damage the war had caused was lack of maintenance.

WESTON PATRICK HOUSE, HAMPSHIRE Above: *Sir Albert Richardson and Eric Houfe's 1956 Classical design perfectly demonstrates that the pre-war Georgian tradition was still going strong.*

ST VEDAST RECTORY, LONDON Right: *Stephen Dykes Bower's Neo-Classical response to Wren.*

PROVOST'S LODGINGS, QUEEN'S COLLEGE, OXFORD Below: *Raymond Erith's deep understanding of architectural context is combined with real originality.*

Sometimes, military occupation had destroyed interiors. Many houses were too big to run economically, and in some cases it was possible to combine a reduction in size with a return to the original form of a house by demolishing Victorian additions.

The work carried out at Meols Hall in Southport, Lancashire, was of a different kind, however. The first of John Cornforth's three articles on the house in *Country Life* in 1973 relates in some detail the complicated story of the Lancashire family of Hesketh and their various houses. For Roger Fleetwood Hesketh (1902–88), who was both the client and the amateur architect, there were three motives for enlarging and rebuilding Meols. One was to provide a home for Mr Hesketh's young family; the second was to house family possessions that he had gathered back together after their dispersal in the 1840s when his ancestor, Sir Peter Fleetwood Hesketh, had lost heart in his speculative development of a new port to rival Liverpool at Fleetwood; and the third was the pleasure of using architecture for symbolic as well as practical purposes.

Roger Hesketh and his brother Peter, close friends of Christopher Hussey, had both studied architecture in the 1920s and travelled widely looking at buildings. They even owned an architecture magazine for a few years in the early 1930s and tried to promote an intelligent, moderate form of Modernism.

Meols is a very convincing evocation of an imaginary past, responding to the precise nuances of early Palladianism in Lancashire. The authentic effect of the seven-bay garden front was increased by reusing salvaged stone from a demolished house by Giacomo Leoni at Lathom House, Ormskirk, and red bricks from Tulketh Hall, Preston – one of several houses that had once belonged to the family. The pair of gazebos at the corners of the garden was based on a similar structure at Rossall, the home of the developer of Fleetwood.

As John Cornforth suggested, the way that Meols was recreated gives insight into the way a country house was conceived in the eighteenth century, often not as a single event leading to a completed building, but as a process of adaptation and growth, in which an architecturally educated patron was often dealing directly with builders rather than with an architect.

Internally, Meols is equally successful. A series of rooms along the garden front was devised to hang family pictures in conjunction with particular pieces of furniture. Although the ceilings are relatively low, the careful study of the dimensions of each object prevented a feeling of overcrowding. It was unusual at the time to hang pictures so close together in the eighteenth-century manner, when the 1930s preference for large blank areas of wall still prevailed. A large single-storey library, appearing as a late-Georgian addition on the entrance front, was scaled so that a magnificent painting of Sir Peter's Arab stallion by James Ward fits between the cornice and the dado at one end, and a Regency bookcase from Bold Hall fills the other end.

Roger Hesketh was MP for Southport until 1959, a job that delayed the execution of his scheme for Meols until he could spend more time at home, and while the reconstruction might suggest simply the diversion of a gentleman amateur architect, it was also a demonstration of confidence in the social contribution that a big house and its farming estate could make to the local community on the edge of a big town.

The building work, which was carefully thought out during the immediate post-war years, was carried out between 1960 and 1964. Although the idea of reconstructing the past may seem odd in contrast with the idea of a forward-looking post-war society, it was an early example of the passion for rescuing old houses that has subsequently become far more widespread in Britain.

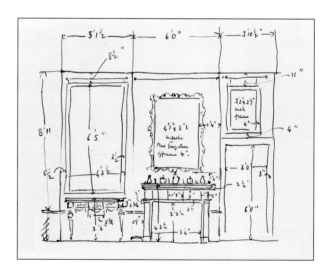

MEOLS HALL, LANCASHIRE Top: *The south front, shown halfway through the process of reconstruction.*

Above: *The main rooms were carefully planned in relation to the picture hanging.*

Right above: *The completed south front is a cleverly contrived historical amalgam, incorporating work from the seventeenth and twentieth centuries.*

Right below: *The entrance front was also largely reconstructed, with the single-storey library on the left.*

FOUR

THE SPACE AGE
1960-70

The typical modern house of the 1950s was characterised by thinness. As a reaction, architects working in the 1960s came to prefer a more substantial look. When colours were used for decoration, they tended to be deeper than the pastels predominant at the Festival of Britain, which had focused public attention on Modernism.

The movement called 'The New Brutalism', which started in the 1950s almost as a private joke, was a reaction against lightness, and in many ways a return to the moral earnestness of the Arts and Crafts movement. Few architects were unaffected by this change of mood, which emphasised the texture of materials.

Ideas about house planning began to change as well. In place of the box-like pavilion structures of the 1950s, whether modern or Classical, came buildings that linked different sections together to accommodate different needs and create a more varied effect.

NO. 3 CHURCH WALK, ALDEBURGH, SUFFOLK
Above: *Nature and culture in harmony.*

THE SPENDER STUDIO, MALDON, ESSEX
Left: *A High-Tech pastoral idyll.*

The architect H. T. ('Jim') Cadbury-Brown (born 1913) worked with Ernö Goldfinger on the design of No. 2 Willow Road before starting his own practice before the war. As his house shows, Goldfinger never followed the 1930s fashion for 'white' architecture, and Cadbury-Brown learnt from him how to use a variety of materials and make each one 'speak'. Later, Cadbury-Brown played an important role in the design of the South Bank exhibition for the Festival of Britain, and went on to design the new buildings for the Royal College of Art next to the Royal Albert Hall.

The architect and his American-born wife, Elizabeth, found a site to build a house in Aldeburgh, Suffolk, in an unusual way. Cadbury-Brown was commissioned by Benjamin Britten and the council of the Aldeburgh Festival to design a small theatre for opera in the plateau-like upper part of the town, but his scheme fell through. This provided the Cadbury-Browns with an opportunity to buy a large plot of land, on which another, smaller house was also built for the musician Imogen Holst, daughter of the composer of *The Planets* and a director of the Festival.

Jim Cadbury-Brown recalls a conversation with Britten, who at the same period liked to use found objects, including on one occasion the springs of an old Rolls-Royce, to provide unusual percussion sounds.

This, they agreed, was the principle adhered to by the Brutalists, whose quest for stimulating asperity the architect compared to the '*brut*' in Champagne *brut*.

No. 3 Church Walk was completed in 1964. It is single-storey and almost invisible from any position until you turn the corner of a gravelled driveway that serves both the houses to discover a partially concealed view of the garden, and a narrow alley between house and garage leading into a courtyard. Entering by the glazed door, one finds oneself on a raised level looking diagonally down on a large living room and, if the kitchen door is open, straight out into the garden. Vistas extend down corridors towards other rooms, and the principle of open planning is tempered by an element of mystery. The sense of enclosure continues with a further courtyard created for the guest bedroom. The Cadbury-Browns created a wild garden beneath the tall pine trees that were already *in situ*, and allowed creeper to cover the walls, almost burying the geometry of the architecture in foliage.

NO. 3 CHURCH WALK, ALDEBURGH, SUFFOLK Below and right: *The simple shapes of the house are used to create courtyards, and the garden continues the series of partly enclosed spaces. The skylights funnel light into internal corridors and rooms.*

The construction of the house, in grey brick, appears simple, but includes unusual details, such as the omission of skirting boards in order that the wall plaster can come right down to the floor, which requires special skill in the plasterer, but is important for creating the effect of a clearly defined space. In a similar spirit, the doors have no architraves, so that the walls are not interrupted with anything to break their sheer surface.

Pieces of furniture, such as bookshelves, stand a little forward from the walls and are raised off the floor for the same reason, while the living room is enlivened by a tall free-standing corner cupboard, the back of which is used for hanging pictures. The furniture combines Victorian and modern pieces, unified by black-leather upholstery and set off by bright lemon-yellow and purple cushions. The simple black, white and grey palette of the brickwork, plaster and tiles never seems oppressive, since areas of garden can be seen from all places in the house, and the simple colours help the bright seaside light to create its own vitality.

One of the virtues of the flat roof is the scope it gives for creating a house with an irregular outline, since pitched roofs work best with controlled geometry. This freedom was not often exploited in the 1950s, but became increasingly prevalent in the 1960s. Skylights mean that the plan can be 'deep', with spaces away from the external walls lit from above. One general aspect of 1960s house planning displayed at No. 3 Church Walk is the development of the courtyard as an alternative to the pavilion. This had become increasingly evident as followers of New Brutalism looked to vernacular precedents in farm-yards and other traditional patterns of settlement. The more contemplative, inward-looking aspect of modern architecture was well served by courtyard plans, which kept the increasingly noisy external world at bay and offered a means of acoustically separating members of households who wanted to 'do their own thing' in terms of radio or television.

Courtyard planning, as demonstrated at Church Walk, also allowed intimate, framed glimpses of nature in the Japanese manner, rather than the bold panoramas seen from the viewing platforms of upper-level living rooms typical of the 1950s. The courtyard house was seen as an appropriate model for urban living, providing privacy and making the best use of the available outdoor space. It was a trend that was promoted in the book *Community and Privacy* by Serge Chermayeff, who began to define some of the basic principles of post-war architecture at Bentley Wood in the mid-1930s, and also taught with Jim Cadbury-Brown at Harvard in the 1950s.

The influence of Frank Lloyd Wright was clearly evident in the design of No. 62 Camden Mews by Edward Cullinan (born 1931). After studying architecture at Cambridge and the Architectural Association in London, Cullinan spent three years on a scholarship in California, where he discovered a proto-modern architecture from the

NO. 3 CHURCH WALK, ALDEBURGH, SUFFOLK *The living room fills the whole of one end of the house, linked to a dining area on a raised platform. Pictures, objects and furniture are arranged with skill and wit.*

early years of the twentieth century, based on wooden construction. Although Wright's work was reasonably well known in Britain, that of his contemporaries, such as Greene and Greene and Bernard Maybeck, was not. Their buildings are full of tactile exposed construction, showing exactly how everything fits together and so creating personality for a building by emphasising its integrity. The influence was not only historical, however. Some of the most positive early signs of 1960s liberation were already apparent in Berkeley in 1956, including the idea that you could build your own house. This sense of the architect as an enabler, rather than a remote expert, has set Cullinan's work apart from many of his contemporaries, while his office has been one of the most influential in the last quarter of the twentieth century in generating new practices from its former staff as well as producing a large number of buildings.

It is perhaps typical of Cullinan that, despite his professional success, he still lives in the house that he originally built forty years ago using his own labour and that of his family and friends to save money. Camden Mews, in North London, slopes from north to south, and is more spaciously planned than many of its equivalents in London. These back sites were favourites for building modern houses or converting existing structures in the post-war period, having a slightly bohemian cachet, as seen in the film *Genevieve*. Camden Mews is in a part of London rougher than Mayfair or Belgravia, but the area is one favoured by architects, with another group of interesting architect-designed houses of the 1960s in Murray Mews, which runs parallel to it behind the opposite side of Camden Square.

The main design decision for the Cullinan house was to place it end-on to the roadway, against the northern site boundary, allowing a strip of clear land to the south, persuading the planners to break with their conventional insistence on a two-storey box with a 10-foot yard in front and behind. There was still very little space, and one of the remarkable aspects of the house is how versatile and inclusive the compact plan was able to be, with a single living space on an upper level, bedrooms and bathroom below, a garage and workshop in the yard, and a terrace garden on its roof.

The main structure is of second-hand London stock brick, with a yard paved in engineering bricks. These were rejects from the Royal College of Physicians in Regent's Park, designed by Sir Denys Lasdun, on which Cullinan was working as an assistant architect while building his own house.

The upper structure is all of timber, apart from its rear wall of brick. It has distinctive overhanging eaves, a feature of later buildings by Cullinan and his followers, and very different in effect from the neat geometry of 1950s Modernist boxes. Cullinan had by this time learnt from experience that without this weather protection, the roof

NO. 62 CAMDEN MEWS, LONDON Above left: *The living room, kitchen and dining room form one continuous space on the upper level.*

Below left: *The colourful ground-floor corridor links the bedrooms.*

Right: *The Cullinan house was ahead of its time in rejecting the standard box solution for a small urban plot.*

structure and the windows below would be at risk. He brought back into architecture a concern for the common-sense aspects of designing for a wet climate that were too often neglected in the desire to create new forms. The timber is bolted together, and the junctions are made between cross pieces, creating a more robust look than normal 'housed' joints, as well as eliminating some of the points where rot can begin. There were only two drawings submitted for planning permission, and as designer and constructor, Cullinan made up a great deal as he went along, claiming that it often takes less time to build something than to draw it.

The tour of the house begins upstairs, after one has climbed steps on to the garage roof. The entrance is in the middle of the south front. In the open-plan room, kitchen and dining area are to the right, with the stairs and sitting area to the left. The solid partitioning is kept down to waist height, for, as Cullinan explains, 'you feel space above your belly button'. The new interest in the processes of food and cookery in the 1960s – also a significant aspect of the Berkeley lifestyle – helped to popularise the farmhouse kitchen style in professional urban homes, with utensils and supplies proudly displayed, and the Cullinan house marks one of the early stages of its penetration. The walls and broad window ledges around the room provide space

CRAY CLEARING, OXFORDSHIRE Top: *The garden side shows the creation of 'outdoor rooms' around the house.*

Above: *The dining room overlooks a pool, with a sculpture by Arthur Pollen, the architect's father, for whom the house was built.*

Left: *Francis Pollen achieved a massive effect with cambered brick walls and a deep eaves overhang.*

for the display of a wide variety of objects, ethnic, Victorian and modern, which are a reminder that such eclecticism in decorative furnishing was also a legacy of the 1960s. The compact planning of the bedrooms downstairs creates the effect of being below decks in a boat, with a similar ingenuity in the use of space, set off with strongly coloured brick walls.

Frank Lloyd Wright's influence appears again at Cray Clearing, Oxfordshire, built by Francis Pollen (1926–87) in 1962. The house was built among the trees of Harpsden Wood above Henley-on-Thames, having been commissioned by the architect's parents, a painter and a sculptor, although he and his family later moved there from The Walled Garden, a house designed by Pollen in the centre of Henley which was featured in *Country Life* in 1960.

Cray Clearing is single-storey, turning away from the view, partly because it was feared that future development would stand in the way. It is, however, an introverted house by temperament, approached by a broad L-shaped courtyard with few windows. One of the distinctive design features is the way that the brick walls, 'battered' in profile to increase their impression of mass, extend forwards from beneath the roof canopy, a clear derivation from Wright's house designs of the 1940s, to create secretive bays of space between the exterior zones and courtyards.

Pollen had begun his architectural career under the spell of Lutyens, partly because his grandfather, Lord Revelstoke, had commissioned the conversion of Lambay Castle in Dublin Bay from Lutyens, and Pollen had spent summer holidays there and met the great man. Starting practice in the early 1950s, Pollen began designing in an overtly Lutyens style, but found in New Brutalism an alternative way of creating the architecture of mass and depth that he desired. Cray Clearing was probably his most successful house; sadly, it was demolished in the mid-1990s in favour of a more conventional house.

Designing a house for one's parents has been the starting point of many great architectural careers. In the case of Creek Vean, near Feock in Cornwall, the design originally involved four architects, one of whom was the client's daughter, although the two male members of Team 4, as their practice was called, namely Richard Rogers (born 1933) and Norman Foster (born 1935), went on to become the two best-known names in British architecture twenty years later. They had met in 1962 on scholarships to study at Yale University, where Serge Chermayeff was one of their tutors. Richard Rogers was accompanied by his wife, Su, and while they were over in the United States heard that Su's father, Marcus Brumwell, a significant figure in the world of design and advertising since the 1930s, was planning to build a retirement home, replacing a nondescript bungalow on the north bank of the creek – a family property since early in the century.

CREEK VEAN, CORNWALL Above left: *The front door is reached across a bridge from the roadside.*

Below left: *A slate staircase gives enticing access to the roof-top.*

Right: *The split levels of the house can be seen from the open well as one moves into the house from the front door to arrive in the studio living room.*

Acting with customary self-confidence, Rogers persuaded his father-in-law to let him design the house instead of his old friend Ernst Freud, the son of Sigmund Freud, who had made some preliminary designs. The prospect of a real job drew Norman Foster back from the United States to set up Team 4 with his wife Wendy and her sister, Georgie Wolton, the only fully qualified member of the team at the outset. The design, which is generally agreed to be a concept by Rogers (although Foster made most of the drawings), was influenced by what the young architects had seen in America, including work by Paul Rudolph, the head of the Yale architecture school, Louis Kahn, one of the visiting professors, and, once more, the pervasive influence of Wright, including in this case his ability to shape a house in relation to a contoured site.

Creek Vean is not quite Fallingwater, but it creates some of the same excitement on approach, with the distant view partly concealed between the two masses of the building. The road is shaded by evergreens, making the contrast between light and dark more telling as one crosses a bridge to enter the house, catching a view of the creek and the Fal estuary beyond, framed between the tall, castle-like living accommodation on the left, and the longer, lower bedroom wing on the right. On the plan, all the room shapes are splayed outwards to the view, with angles reflected in the plan. A broadening

CREEK VEAN, CORNWALL Above: *The gallery provided a hanging wall for some of the Brumwells' exceptional collection of twentieth-century art. Bedrooms open off, with wide sliding doors.*

Left: *The kitchen-dining room has a simple island kitchen unit in steel, designed by Su Rogers. One whole wall is glazed and looks out over the creek and estuary beyond.*

flight of grassy steps descends to the narrow terrace of garden, with the grandeur of a civic building in miniature.

The entrance level leads into a sitting area formed as a broad balcony over the kitchen-dining room below. Here the Brumwells hung some of the paintings from their notable collection of 1930s artists, all of them personal friends. These included works painted by Ben Nicholson and his wife, Winifred, when they first discovered Cornwall in 1927, staying as guests of the Brumwells in the farmhouse on the opposite side of the creek. The construction of the house was largely financed by the sale of a painting by Piet Mondrian, which Marcus Brumwell had bought from the artist at the end of the 1930s to help him pay his rent before leaving for New York.

The exposed concrete blocks that provide both interior and exterior walls are pale in tone, contrasted with the dark Delabole slate which provides the flooring, adding a sense of solidity usually found in old vernacular buildings. The painted surfaces were kept to a minimum, and the slate floors meant that chronic leaks in the roof could simply be mopped up. A novel aspect of the planning is the way that big sliding doors open up one side of the bedrooms along the corridor, which was designed as a picture gallery with skylights overhead. When the sliding doors are open, the house can seem much larger, with bookshelving and picture-hanging extending from one space to another. At the end of the gallery, a glazed door extends the space by framing a different and more intimate external view.

The problems of working with conventional solid construction at Creek Vean, and in a pair of houses in Murray Mews, Camden Town, at the outset of his career, stimulated Richard and Su Rogers' interest in alternative methods of construction that could make the process of house building quicker and less dependent on individual contractors. Ever since the 1920s, the partially prefabricated 'unit' house had exercised a fascination for architects hoping to emulate the production efficiency of the motor industry. The American designer and inventor Buckminster Fuller had tried without success to launch his Dymaxion house on the market, but remained an inspiration to a younger generation, including Foster and Rogers, who went on to develop the High-Tech Movement.

THE SPENDER STUDIO, MALDON, ESSEX Right: *The structural steel frame, painted yellow, dominates the interior and exterior. All windows are on two opposite faces of the house, and all run from floor to ceiling.*

Below: *Humphrey Spender's working studio can be seen across the garden, in a matching building. The living room runs from one side of the house to the other, filled with objects that seem anything but High-Tech.*

In 1964, while occupied with Creek Vean, Richard and Su Rogers met Humphrey Spender, an artist, photographer and textile designer who had himself trained as an architect, and discussed how house building might be made more efficient. Three years later, wishing to build a new house and studio in the garden of his Victorian house at Ulting, near Maldon in Essex, Spender contacted the Rogerses again. They embarked on a building project with numerous frustrations and pitfalls, which produced a delightful house without achieving any breakthrough in cost, speed or efficiency, since the builders and suppliers were not ready to change their ways.

The principle was to use a standard steel portal truss, strong enough to support a roof over the whole width of the house. This was emphasised in the Modern Movement manner by appearing clearly legible, in bright yellow, outside the walls. A service core in the centre of the plan left two complete runs of glazing, with the two other walls filled in solid. The Spender Studio, which was begun in 1968 and completed two years later, consists of a house with a separate studio

and carport forming a sort of gatehouse. Set in an old orchard, it still offers, as intended, a seductive model for urban living with private outdoor space, and a similar house was built in Wimbledon for Rogers' parents before he moved on to greater things with the Centre Pompidou in Paris.

In the political climate of the 1960s, the idea of building private houses was often seen among architects to be self-indulgent when so much effort was being expended on public housing. One justification often used was that, as with the Spender Studio, experiments made in the private sector could later be applied for the benefit of the masses. Hal Higgins (born 1926) and Reyner Ney (born 1928), the architects of Heathbrow in Hampstead (1959–61), were prominent in moving housing design on from the stereotypical slab block and tower block. They introduced more complex planning, in which housing became less like an object distinct from its surroundings, and more like an inseparable combination of accommodation and urban landscape, seen in schemes like St Peter's Terrace in Reporton Road, Fulham.

The commentary in *Country Life* by John Rae emphasised Heathbrow's Romantic and Picturesque qualities: 'One explores the house rather than walking through it, and is kept interested, as in an eighteenth-century landscape garden, by the opening up, and closing

again, of spaces and views.'¹ As with many houses of this period, the entrance presents a slightly forbidding blankness, although the approach is carefully landscaped. The lower-ground level, extending in line with the entrance pathway and dug back into the slope of the hill, was given over to children, while an open stair by the front door ascends to the large living room, with distant views over Hampstead Heath. Behind this room are the kitchen and dining room, each with an outdoor terrace. John Rae also pointed out the unity of conception in the furnishings, all of which were chosen by the architects, comparing this to nearby Kenwood, with its interiors by Robert Adam. The critic Ian Nairn described Heathbrow in 1964 as 'a simple, quiet brick house built with absolute assurance in the details and the volumes: one of the most powerful new buildings in London'.² The house is now the Embassy of Croatia.

The list of clients for modern houses in the 1960s can be as interesting as the list of architects. Restoring an older house was still not an attractive choice for many people, partly because there were fewer architects and builders with appropriate experience than in later years. Construction costs were relatively stable in the early 1960s, and only began to rise sharply at the end of the decade and beyond. Building was therefore once more an adventure that for many clients represented a personal statement of values, as it had been in the 1920s and 1930s, and not just the investment of wealth in prestige. House prices increased steadily, but houses were not then seen primarily as tradeable assets and secondarily as homes, as they often are today. One might not, in today's cultural climate, find a popular entertainer commissioning a new house from a young architectural practice with results that provoke a serious article in *Country Life*, as Max Bygraves did in the 1960s.

PENTICE WALK, SURREY Above: *The lounge on the ground floor connects through folding doors to a study beyond. A separate living and dining room was provided in the rear wing, facing west.*

Left: *Pentice Walk was designed for Max Bygraves by Sherban Cantacuzino. The upper rooms are linked by a pergola-like walkway.*

Sherban Cantacuzino (born 1928), who was the partner of Steane, Shipman and Cantacuzino chiefly involved in the job, recalls that Max Bygraves chose his architects with advice from the RIBA. He wanted a modern house, but not too modern, and it was therefore given a pitched roof and plenty of timber to create a Scandinavian effect. Cantacuzino persuaded him to have the external access balcony running around two sides of the L-shaped house, which gave it the name 'Pentice Walk', after the medieval device of a pentice (a lean-to sheltered structure giving access usually to the upper level of a house which lacked internal stairs). In the Bygraves house, it becomes an architectural ordering device recalling Chermayeff's Bentley Wood (see pages 86–9), a house that Cantacuzino included in his book *Modern Houses of the World* (1964). For a house with a lot of south-facing glazing, the balcony also helps to give shade in the summer, while allowing the low winter sun to come right into the rooms; it is a design device increasingly found in present-day buildings.

The long, low line of the house is counterpointed by the pyramid roof of the garage with a playroom overhead, reached by a bridge branching off from the 'pentice walk', a space that Bygraves also saw as a bolthole for his own use. On the flat site, the composition, formed by contrasting volumes, seems to suggest a connection with Cantacuzino's explanation of architecture as a formal art, 'concerned with such abstract notions as the organisation of forms in space and the relationships of the different parts to each other and to the whole'. He goes on to compare the experience of this in architecture to 'the sort of pleasure in observing a skill that one has from following the performance of contrapuntal music with a score'.[3]

The idea of composing a house as a set of discrete volumes, as seen at Pentice Walk, has a long ancestry, including the villas of Andrea

ARUNDEL PARK, SUSSEX Above: *Arundel Park was one of the largest Classical houses of its time, built for the Duke and Duchess of Norfolk by Claud Phillimore as an experiment in adapting the three-part Palladian plan to modern needs.*

Left: *The drawing room was decorated by John Fowler, adding richness to a simple architectural frame.*

Palladio in northern Italy and their derivatives in Britain and other parts of the world. For Palladio, the villa was a self-contained building with its own compositional rules, but, taking his lead from certain Roman remains, he understood the opportunity of enhancing its impressiveness by linking smaller buildings, usually for purposes of farming, to the centre in a symmetrical composition. It is surprising how long and deeply the Victorian prejudice against Palladio lasted.

Publications by historians such as Christopher Hussey, John Summerson, Rudolf Wittkower and James Lees-Milne in the early 1950s produced a complete reversal of opinion, and Palladio quickly acquired the status of an architect of first rank, with a corresponding reappraisal of English Palladianism. The architect Claud Phillimore (1911–94) had his own connection to Palladio, however, for he inherited one of the most inventive and complex Palladio villas, the Villa Foscari, 'La Malcontenta', from Bertie Landsberg, a South American who rescued it from dereliction. Phillimore was one of a handful of architects working in the post-war years almost exclusively for the landed gentry, building houses in a traditional style.

The Duchess of Norfolk met him when visiting a tuberculosis hospital at Midhurst, Sussex, where Phillimore was a patient. As John Martin Robinson described in *Country Life* in 1996, 'he had spent his convalescence dreaming of plans for an "ideal house", which would revive the Palladian concept of a main block and flankers, but would be adapted for convenient modern living'.[4] This coincided with the Duchess's scheme to build a new dower house in the park at Arundel in order to have greater privacy than she and her husband, the 16th Duke, could find at Arundel Castle itself.

Arundel Park, the new house, was begun in 1958 and completed in 1962. The overall configuration of a centre block and pavilion wings is immediately recognisable, but the centre is not an imitation Palladio villa, being more Regency in style, with deep Italianate eaves and projecting semicircular bows over the entrance and at each end of the south front. The style of roof is echoed in the wings, providing staff accommodation, the whole house being festively colour-washed in pink, and topped by a cupola and railed walkway more typical of the seventeenth century.

Phillimore was used to economising for his patrons, and none of his houses use much architectural detail on the exterior. Internally, Arundel Park has less architectural ornament than most houses of the period that it evokes. Where ornament is found, it is often in the form of salvaged doors or chimneypieces from elsewhere, although the wrought-iron stair rail is a fine piece of craftsmanship. As furnished by the 16th Duke, with items taken from Arundel Castle and arranged by John Fowler, Arundel Park achieved an appropriate level of grandeur, even though the ceiling heights are relatively low.

Classical country-house work was not often published in the 1960s, even in *Country Life*, which would not have excluded it on grounds of style. It is likely that owners of the grander, newly built houses did not wish to draw attention to themselves, either for reasons of good manners or from fear of unwelcome intrusion. Phillimore's work remains relatively unknown, as does that of T. A. Bird (who by

SUNDERLANDWICK, YORKSHIRE Top: *Francis Johnson replaced a destroyed house with a new one, designed to form a unity with the surviving Victorian stable block.*

Above: *The hall and passageways were designed with careful consideration of the fall of light.*

LUSHILL HOUSE, WILTSHIRE Left: *The staircase hall, by T. A. Bird, is a highly accomplished variation on a late-Georgian theme.*

HENBURY HALL, CHESHIRE   Above: *A vista of Kentian doorcases carved by Dick Reid of York. The interior design is by David Mlinaric.*

Left: *The staircase departs from Palladian precedent by filling one corner of the square plan. The shaping of the underside of each cantilevered stone step makes a spectacular pattern.*

exponents of traditional architecture and made their work more
visible.

Ashfold was built for Mr Simpson's parents and grew slowly, from
the first drawings in 1985 to completion in 1991. The house is a
symptom not just of the Classical Revival, but of the revival of
interest in Sir John Soane, whose austere, abstracted Classicism was
being claimed as an inspiration by an increasing number of architects
of many countries – Modernists, Post-Modernists and Classicists
alike. The obvious references to Soane at Ashfold come in allusions to
his houses at Pitzhanger Manor, Ealing, and Lincoln's Inn Fields, but
also in a more adventurous sense of internal space than is found in
other Classical Revival houses. This aspect of Ashfold helps to
overcome the relatively small dimensions, and it extends into the
meticulous design of hidden cupboards and closets all over the house.

As at Lincoln's Inn Fields, what appear to be solid walls reveal
themselves as hinged doors, so that in a modern house the clutter of
advanced electronic devices does not obstruct the view. Simpson
introduced similar features into his design for the Queen's Gallery at
Buckingham Palace, which opened in 2002.

While the other Classical architects surveyed in this chapter have
worked with interior decorators, or left the furnishing in the hands of
the client, Simpson shares with Francis Johnson (see pages 151–4) a
passionate interest in the design of everything relating to the interior.
As in the 1930s, architects and collectors in the 1980s were fascinated
by the Regency, particularly in its more theatrical and bizarre mani-
festations, and Ashfold includes a mixture of antiques and newly
created pieces, including a matching Empire sofa and chaise longue
in the drawing room, and heavier seating in the library.

ASHFOLD HOUSE, SUSSEX Above: *John Simpson's clean and elegant house for his*
parents is above all a homage to Sir John Soane.

Left: *The staircase rising through the centre of the plan is one of the most spatially*
exciting works of new Classicism from the 1980s.

SIX

DIFFERING VIEWS

1990–2000

'To build in a contemporary manner in the rural landscape
of the late twentieth century is to risk public contempt,'
wrote Marcus Field when presenting Baggy House to readers of
Country Life in September 1996; but this house was a portent
of change.[1] Architects had learned to become more accommodating
and were more attuned to the demands of a consumer society.
That same year, the Conservative minister for environment,
John Gummer, introduced PPG7, a clause in planning guidance
that encouraged local authorities to grant permission to build
substantial country houses of exceptional design quality.
The apparent dominance of Classicism in the 1980s was being
modified by other possibilities, none of them
genuinely new, but indicative, perhaps, of a change of mood.
The revival of modern architecture was about to begin
all over again.

BAGGY HOUSE, DEVON Above: *The breakfast corner in the kitchen.*
Left: *Hand-painted curtains shade a dazzling view of the sea.*

With less than ten years' hindsight, no house could be more representative of its exact historical moment than Baggy House. The client, Gavyn Davies, is a London banker and a supporter of New Labour. The magnificent coastal site contained an old hotel, partly Victorian and partly Art Deco, and the architect, Anthony Hudson, began by exploring the possibility of converting it, but advised instead in favour of demolition and rebuilding. While no new house would have received planning permission on this site, a replacement was deemed acceptable, and the white render of the new house recalled the general appearance of its Art Deco predecessor. Baggy House conveys the same message of confidence that Quinlan Terry's Classical houses gave ten years earlier, but reflects the achievement of modern architecture in regaining its entitlement to be the bearer of such messages.

No longer promoted as a purgative medicine, Modernism became a lifestyle choice in the 1990s, and designers made sure that it was glossy-looking, photogenic and capable of producing a good story. Baggy House looks immediately interesting from afar, but the fun really begins inside the front door, with a great variety of forms and materials, including a monolithic column of granite supporting a lead-clad ceiling in the hall. The main living space is arranged as a set of

levels commanding the seaward view through a corner window reminiscent of Frank Lloyd Wright, with a tapered column of maple wood acting as a vertical marker. The upper level is for relaxed sitting, or lounging, in a variety of 'designer' chairs, while below, a glass-topped table, designed by the architect to have a rough texture and colour, provides the centrepiece of the dining area.

Translucent curtains in raw silk, hand-painted by Louise Woodward, hang across the windows, which can be lowered out of sight. Further well-chosen details of contemporary craft and design make Baggy House as representative of its own time as any house of the Adam or Arts and Crafts periods. If the design seems to be trying to do too many things at once, then it could be excused for celebrating a sense of release after Modernism's years in the wilderness.

During the early 1990s, people began to talk about 'bungalow eating'. This was partly a solution to the high costs of building a new house, but even more it was a way of getting around planning

BAGGY HOUSE, DEVON Above: *Anthony Hudson's design is based on a composition of interlocking volumes, making a building that encourages viewing in the round in its exposed position.*

Right: *The relationship to a view has always been an important aspect of Modernist design.*

restrictions. Bungalow eating could involve razing an existing house to the ground but reconnecting to the original services, or it could be a slightly less radical transformation of an existing structure to improve its architectural character.

Roderick Gradidge (1929–2000), a vociferous opponent of Modernism, managed this process with considerable skill. He even wrote an operetta, *Grey Roses*, about recovering an imaginary Lutyens house from layers of unsympathetic later additions. The two Gradidge houses in Surrey and Sussex, published together in a *Country Life* article by Michael Hall in 1998, were neither of them strictly bungalows, and neither was completely consumed in the process of transformation, but each received a new wing, with the opportunity to alter the plan and create new spaces. The New House retained its multiple gables along the entrance side, but these were tile-hung, and the original service end of the house was incorporated in a new wing

with guest accommodation above, and a new dining room with an inglenook fireplace below.

Perhaps the most evocative image from the pair of houses comes from The Old Rectory, where a double-height room for entertaining and concerts was added to the dull Neo-Georgian house of 1958 by Christopher Green. Its positioning, with a tall window at one end overlooking the garden, is reminiscent of a similar room by Lutyens at Le Bois des Moutiers, the house near Dieppe that he designed in 1900. The light fitting, designed by Gradidge, is typical of the architect's love of the more demonstrative decorative objects of the turn of the century.

Among the traditional designers practising quietly in the 1980s was Charles Morris (born 1943). It is not correct to call him an architect, for his qualification is as a surveyor and such a misnomer is contrary to the Architects' Registration Act; however, since the early 1970s he has been operating in all but name as an architect, designing and supervising the construction of buildings of varied scale. Most of these have been rural and domestic, although Morris has also designed a striking golf clubhouse near Leeds. As Jeremy Musson wrote in *Country Life* in 1999, 'although largely unnoticed by the mainstream architectural press, in future decades [Morris's] name

THE NEW HOUSE, SURREY Above: *An existing house transformed by Roderick Gradidge in the style of the turn-of-the-century Arts and Crafts movement. He particularly enjoyed making three-dimensional compositions from traditional tiled roofs.*

THE OLD RECTORY, SUSSEX Left: *The Great Room by Roderick Gradidge mixes old and new parts of a 1950s house to dramatic effect, with a large groin-vaulted ceiling and a Picturesque balcony overlooking from the adjacent upper-floor landing.*

will pepper the index of artists and the footnotes of revised editions of Pevsner's *Buildings of England*.[2]

Dunesslin, Dumfriesshire, published in *Country Life* in 2000, represents the same circularity as the work of Roderick Gradidge in its return to the forms and principles of the Arts and Crafts movement of a century before. It is an extension of an existing house, picking up the local style as an architect of 1900 might have done. At the core was a farmhouse of 1786, with an earlier and smaller wing to the rear, to which Morris has attached a new tower, providing guest accommodation with a large study at the top. The difficulty in adding to a vernacular building of this kind is to capture the kind of skilled but not over-calculating workmanship of the past. Only a rare workman today can be trusted to improvise on site in order to let the materials speak.

Inside the wing connecting the two main parts of the enlarged house, Morris formed a Great Room, screened from the entrance hall by the dumpy columns that are one of his signature elements. The thin Roman bricks of the fire recess are similar to those used by Lutyens, and the overmantel is in the Scottish vernacular tradition, in which a sunken quatrefoil holds a projecting lozenge with the date of the new work.

One category of design that, since the late 1960s, has come closest to holding a central position is not representative of a style, but of the concern for saving energy and materials. 'Green', 'ecological' and 'sustainable' are more or less interchangeable terms for this kind of architecture, and the results come in many forms, frequently built of timber and designed to make the best use of solar energy. Often the application of sustainable solutions produces forms almost indistinguishable from vernacular ones, favouring traditional local

DUNESSLIN, DUMFRIESSHIRE Above: *The link block is the oldest part, with the extended 1786 farmhouse to the right. Charles Morris's addition of a tower makes a satisfying composition that leaves the earlier parts intact.*

Right: *The Great Room was formed on the ground floor of the link building with simple solid detailing.*

materials to minimise transport, while avoiding most manufactured materials, including metals and plastics, because of the high levels of 'embodied energy' accumulated in the processes that converted them from their raw state.

Thus at Westlake Brake in Devon, designed by David Sheppard (born 1960), the walls are made of rammed earth, a traditional method of solid walling that has enjoyed a gradual revival. Earth walling, usually in cob, is commonly found in Devon, as the clay in the local soil favours it. On this occasion, the material for the walls was the by-product of excavating the foundations. The wisdom of solid walls in the past was that they could act as 'heat sinks', absorbing heat by day and releasing it at night – qualities not obtainable in a modern cavity wall. A further cooling element is provided by a pond within the house, fed with fresh water from a culvert. In the centre of the house is a large area of glass, distinctly modern in character, where desert plants are grown, and the living quarters at the two ends of the house are joined by a bridge. Recycling materials is another important aspect of green architecture; here, the central support for the spiral staircase is made from an old telegraph pole.

There could apparently be no greater contrast between Charles Morris's Dunesslin and the two small houses by Jonathan Ellis-Miller

WESTLAKE BRAKE, DEVON Top: *The main living spaces of the house are at the upper level in two wings, connected by a bridge across the greenhouse in the centre of the house* (above).

Left: *The house enjoys 200-degree panoramic views of the sea. The rammed-earth walls are of typical red Devon clay.*

(born 1962), at Prickwillow near Ely, Cambridgeshire, on the edge of the Fens, but both results represent a designer reviving an existing tradition with personal enjoyment and conviction. In our pluralist age, we may finally have come to believe that in order for one of them to be right, the other does not have to be wrong.

The house that Ellis-Miller built for himself in the late 1980s at No. 1A Kingdon Avenue looked back to a specific moment and place: the lightweight steel Case Study Houses in California in the 1950s, mentioned in Chapter 3. Like much of the modern architecture of the last years of the twentieth century, it was as much involved in historical reference as Classicism. One of the closest equivalents in Britain would be the Spender Studio, but in place of the heavy steel, there was a lighter frame and white everywhere.

It was appropriate and not accidental that No. 1B Kingdon Avenue should be built as a house and studio for Mary Banham, the widow of the architectural critic and historian Reyner Banham, who was an enthusiast for Los Angeles and for the Case Study Houses. The mutual contact was the architect John Winter, a friend of Reyner Banham's since childhood, and the former employer of Ellis-Miller, whom he advised when the first house was being built. Mrs Banham's studio, built in the late 1990s, was an improved and slightly enlarged

version of the Ellis-Miller house, raised off the ground by a couple of feet and taller from floor to ceiling. This is a workplace, with a studio glazed all around to collect the bright East Anglian light. The configurations of the rooms can be altered with pivoting screens, a feature of many Modern Movement houses.

Modern houses can become national news events, indicating that many more people would dream of owning one than their detractors might assume. If Prickwillow is a rather unexpected place to find them, then the village of Highgate, long absorbed into London, is more predictable, since it already has the Tayler and Green Studio and the Leonard Manasseh house at No. 6 Bacons Lane, among several other notable examples of modern architecture. Manasseh, indeed, comes into the story of The Lawns, which overlooks his own house and garden, and has even more spectacular views over London. It is built on the basement of a Victorian house, from which it takes

---

NO. 1B KINGDON AVENUE, PRICKWILLOW, CAMBRIDGESHIRE
Right: *Mary Banham's studio house is one of a pair of modern houses by Jonathan Ellis-Miller.*

NO. 1A KINGDON AVENUE, PRICKWILLOW, CAMBRIDGESHIRE
Below: *The sitting room of Jonathan Ellis-Miller's own house, in the tradition of lightweight American Modernism.*

its name, which was bought by Manasseh, who divided its garden into separate plots, one of which contains his own house.

As seen today, The Lawns is a house built by Manasseh as a more convenient replacement for its Victorian predecessor, and then transformed by the architects Nick Eldridge (born 1957) and Piers Smerin (born 1962), whose initial proposal was selected by the clients, designers John and Frances Sorrell, because they liked the idea of its layers of building. For the planners at Camden Council, the concept proved less alarming than a complete rebuilding. An extra space was added to the entrance front, making the whole experience of entering a more generous one. At the top of the house is a studio, replacing the pitched roof, which was added in the 1980s to the Manasseh house, contained within a glass box whose white floor adds to the sense of floating in the clouds on the roof of London.

The south side of the house is organised with an enfilade of connecting rooms, from a large kitchen at one end, stepping down through a dining room and central living room to a conservatory overlooking a courtyard garden, with a water sculpture by William Pye. The shapes of the original windows were retained, but the house was extended to each side, becoming more like a Palladian villa translated into modern terms. In the living room, the white walls over the fireplace open at the touch of a button, revealing that the secret of minimalist living is to have plenty of hidden storage space. The Victorian basement still does good service in providing a much less visually perfect realm inhabited by the Sorrells' teenage children, who can emerge into the light from time to time for feeding and laundering.

One probably should not try to draw lessons from any single example. The Lawns was completed in 2000, making it a convenient stopping point. Metaphorically, it might suggest that English houses are seldom free from history, and that this history goes around in circles more often than it goes along in straight lines.

THE LAWNS, LONDON Above: *The outline of the original 1950s house by Leonard Manasseh is still apparent on the south front, with the 2000 additions by Eldridge and Smerin of the roof-top studio and the conservatory and kitchen to either side.*

Left: *The kitchen is completely integrated into the rest of the house.*

NOTES

INTRODUCTION

1. I am aware that use of the term 'Britain' is contentious, but it is adopted because Scotland and Wales are represented in the selection of examples.

2. H. S. Goodhart-Rendel, Address at the Bristol Conference of the RIBA, *Architect and Building News*, 24 June 1938, p.393.

3. R. Randal Phillips, 'Some Houses at Silver End Garden Village, Essex', *Country Life*, 27 October 1928, p.601.

4. *Ibid.*

5. 'Design for Living', *Country Life*, 20 May 1933, p.512.

6. Christopher Hussey, 'High and Over', *Country Life*, 19 September 1931, p.302.

7. Reginald Blomfield, *Modernismus: A Study*, Macmillan, London, 1934, pp.79–80.

8. John Summerson, 'Romance and Realities', *Country Life* [supplement], 13 February 1937, pp.ii–iii.

9. Oliver Brooke, 'Wanted: A Style', *Country Life*, 1 December 1934, p.598.

10. Evelyn Waugh, 'A Call to the Orders', *Country Life* [supplement], 26 February 1938, reprinted in *The Essays, Articles and Reviews of Evelyn Waugh*, edited by Donat Gallagher, Methuen, London, 1983, p.216.

11. Lionel Brett, *The Things We Look At: Houses*, Penguin Books, Harmondsworth, 1947, p.38.

12. Arthur Oswald, 'The Modern House, A Survey of the Past Twenty-Five Years', *Country Life*, 23 September 1939, p.317.

13. John Summerson, 'Houses of Twenty Years', *Country Life*, 12 October 1940, p.332.

14. Arthur Oswald, 'Great Swifts, Cranbrook, Kent', *Country Life*, 18 November 1939, p.528; Christopher Hussey, 'Godmersham Park, Kent', *Country Life*, 16 and 23 February and 2 March 1945, pp.288–91, 332–5, 376–9; 'The Re-Building of Castle Hill, Devon', *Country Life*, 29 October 1938, pp.426–30.

15. Arthur Oswald, 'A Modern House in the Regency Tradition: Landhurst, Hartfield, Sussex', *Country Life*, 18 February 1949, pp.366–8.

16. R. Randal Phillips, 'An Architect's Own House', *Country Life*, 7 November 1938, pp.xliv–xlviii; R. Randal Phillips, 'Women as Architects', *Country Life*, 27 May 1939, pp.564–5.

17. Extracts from Campbell's theoretical writings are reproduced in Alan Powers, *John Campbell: The Rediscovery of an Arts and Crafts Architect*, Prince of Wales's Institute of Architecture, London, 1997.

18. See *Country Life*, 23 October 1958, pp.944–5.

19. Planning Policy Guidance Note 7, 1996, Section 3.21. Source: ODPM website, April 2004.

CHAPTER 1

1. Philip Tilden, *True Remembrances*, Country Life Books, London, 1954, p.42.

2. 'A Group of Houses at West Byfleet, Surrey', *Country Life*, 9 April 1921, pp.447–8.

3. John Cornforth, 'Shepherd's Hill, Sussex', *Country Life*, 9 October 1975, p.909.

4. For a fuller description of Mulberry House, see John Cornforth's earlier volume in this series, *London Interiors: From the Archives of Country Life*, Aurum Press, London, 2000, pp.28–32.

5. Christopher Hussey, 'Gayfere House, Westminster', *Country Life*, 13 February 1932, p.180.

CHAPTER 2

1. Christopher Hussey, 'High Cross Hill', *Country Life*, 11 February 1933, p.147.

2. *Ibid*, p.149.

3. Christopher Hussey, 'Yaffle Hill, Dorset', *Country Life*, 8 July 1933, p.17.

4. Christopher Hussey, 'Eltham Hall, Kent', *Country Life*, 29 May 1937, p.597.

5. Quoted in Clive Aslet, 'An Interview with the late Paul Paget', *Thirties Society Journal*, No. 6, 1987, p.22.

6. Osbert Lancaster, *Homes Sweet Homes*, John Murray, London, 1939, p.74.

7. Michael Hall, 'Gribloch, Stirlingshire', *Country Life*, 12 February 1998, p.57.

8. Christopher Hussey, 'Birchens Spring, Beaconsfield', *Country Life*, 20 January 1938, p.114.

9. John Campbell, 'The Portal Houses: Principles Involved', *Builder*, 15 September 1944, pp.214–15.

10. Quoted in Christopher Hussey, 'Ridgemead, Englefield Green', *Country Life*, 17 February 1940, p.176.

11. Quoted by Michael Powers, the author's father, who visited The Homewood in 1939.

CHAPTER 3

1. R. Randal Phillips, *Houses for Moderate Means*, 3rd edn, Country Life Books, London, 1949, p.6.

2. H. Dalton Clifford, 'Architect's Home in Blackheath', *Country Life*, 31 July 1958, p.239.

3. Mark Girouard, 'Keeping the Children Under', *Country Life*, 12 November 1959, p.830.

4. *Architectural Review*, December 1955, p.365.

5. Mark Girouard, 'House that Juts Over a Valley', *Country Life*, 11 February 1960, p.284.

6. *Ibid*, p.286.

7. Mark Girouard, 'Architectural Scholarship at Oxford', *Country Life*, 7 July 1960, p.34.

8. Lucy Archer, *Raymond Erith, Architect*, Cygnet Press, Burford, 1985, p.65.

CHAPTER 4

1. John Rae, 'A House Built as a Unity', *Country Life*, 9 May 1963, p.1053.

2. Ian Nairn, *Modern Buildings in London*, London Transport, London, 1964, p.43.

3. Sherban Cantacuzino, *Modern Houses of the World*, Studio Vista, London, 1964, pp.7–8.

4. John Martin Robinson, 'Arundel Park, Sussex', *Country Life*, 20 June 1996, p.62.

5. Clive Aslet, 'Bentley Farm, Sussex', *Country Life*, 13 September 1984, p.695.

6. John Cornforth, 'King's Walden Bury, Hertfordshire', *Country Life*, 27 September 1973, p.858.

CHAPTER 5

1. Aldington and Craig, 'Understanding People and Developing a Brief', in Byron Mikellides, *Architecture for People*, Studio Vista, London, 1980, p.28.

2. Giles Worsley, 'Pillwood, Feock, Cornwall', *Country Life*, 7 August 2003, p.44.

3. Clive Aslet, 'Barley Splatt, Cornwall', *Country Life*, 30 May 1985, p.1495.

4. Clive Aslet, 'The New House, Sussex', *Country Life*, 17 July 1986, p.164.

5. David Watkin, 'Merks Hall, Essex', *Country Life*, 7 July 1988, p.142.

6. John Martin Robinson, *The Latest Country Houses*, The Bodley Head, London, 1984, p.192.

CHAPTER 6

1. Marcus Field, 'Baggy House, Devon', *Country Life*, 26 September 1996, p.75.

2. Jeremy Musson, 'Paperhouse, Norfolk', *Country Life*, 14 October 1999, p.56.

BIBLIOGRAPHY

PERIOD SOURCES

Before 1939

Abercrombie, Patrick (ed.), *The Book of the Modern House*, Waverley Book Company, London, 1939.

Anon., *The Smaller House*, Architectural Press, London, 1924.

Carrington, Noel, *Design in the Home*, Country Life Books, London, 1933.

Carter, Ella, *Seaside Houses and Bungalows*, Country Life Books, London, 1937.

Chatterton, Frederick, *Small Houses and Bungalows*, Architectural Press, London, 1932.

Cresswell, H. B., *The Honeywood File: An Adventure in Building*, Faber & Faber, London, 1929.

—, *The Honeywood Settlement: A Continuation of the Honeywood File*, Faber & Faber, London, 1930.

James, C. H. and Yerbury, F. R., *Modern English Houses and Interiors*, Ernest Benn, London, 1925.

Lancaster, Osbert, *Pillar to Post: A Pocket Lamp of Architecture*, John Murray, London, 1938.

—, *Homes Sweet Homes*, John Murray, London, 1939.

Marshall, H. G. Hayes, *Interior Decoration To-Day*, Frank Lewis, Leigh-on-Sea, 1938.

McGrath, Raymond, *Twentieth Century Houses*, Faber & Faber, London, 1934.

Miller, Duncan, *Interior Decorating*, The Studio, London, 1937.

Myerscough-Walker, R., *Choosing a Modern House*, The Studio, London, 1939.

Patmore, Derek, *Modern Furnishing and Decoration*, The Studio, London, 1934.

—, *Decoration for the Small Home*, Putnam, London, 1938.

Phillips, R. Randal, *The Modern English House*, Country Life Books, London, [1927].

—, *The Modern English Interior*, Country Life Books, London, [1928].

Schrijver, Herman, *Decoration for the Home*, Frank Lewis, Leigh-on-Sea, 1939.

Smithells, Roger, *Modern Small Country Houses*, Country Life Books, London, 1936.

Yerbury, F. R., *Small Modern English Houses*, Victor Gollancz, London, 1929.

Yorke, F. R. S., *The Modern House*, Architectural Press, London, 1934.

—, *The Modern House in England*, Architectural Press, London, 1937 (2nd edn published 1944).

After 1939

Brett, Lionel, *The Things We See: Houses*, Penguin, Harmondsworth, 1947.

Clifford, H. Dalton, *New Houses for Moderate Means*, Country Life Books, London, 1957.

Crosby, Theo and Pidgeon, Monica, *An Anthology of Houses*, B. T. Batsford, London, 1960.

Hope, Alice, *Town Houses*, B. T. Batsford, London, 1963.

The House Book, Phaidon, London, 2001.

Penn, Colin, *Houses for Today*, B. T. Batsford, London, 1954.

Whiting, Penelope, *New Houses*, Architectural Press, London, 1964.

HISTORICAL SURVEYS

Airs, Malcolm (ed.), *The Twentieth Century Great House*, Oxford University Department for Continuing Education, Oxford, 2002.

Aslet, Clive, *The Last Country Houses*, Yale University Press, London, 1982.

— and Powers, Alan, *The National Trust Book of the English House*, Viking/Penguin, London, 1985.

Battersby, Martin, *The Decorative Twenties*, Studio Vista, London, 1969.

—, *The Decorative Thirties*, Studio Vista, London, [1971].

Calloway, Stephen, *Twentieth Century Decoration*, Weidenfeld & Nicolson, London, 1988.

Cantacuzino, Sherban, *Modern Houses of the World*, Studio Vista, London, 1964.

Cornforth, John, *The Inspiration of the Past: Country House Taste in the Twentieth Century*, Viking, London, 1985.

—, *The Search for a Style: Country Life and Architecture, 1897–1935*, André Deutsch, London, 1988.

—, *London Interiors: From the Archives of Country Life*, Aurum Press, London, 2000.

Garland, Madge, *The Indecisive Decade: The World of Fashion and Entertainment in the Thirties*, Macdonald, London, 1968.

Gradidge, Roderick, *Dream Houses: The Edwardian Ideal*, Constable, London, 1980.

Harwood, Elain, *England: A Guide to Post-War Listed Buildings*, 2nd edn, B. T. Batsford, London, 2003.

Jackson, Lesley, *'Contemporary': Architecture and Interiors of the 1950s*, Phaidon, London, 1994.

—, *The Sixties: Decade of Design Revolution*, London, Phaidon, 1998.

Powers, Alan (ed.), *Real Architecture*, The Building Centre, London, 1987.

Robinson, John Martin, *The Latest Country Houses*, The Bodley Head, London, 1984.

Twentieth Century Architecture 2: The Modern House Revisited, The Twentieth Century Society, London, 1996.

Twentieth Century Architecture 4: The Post-War House, The Twentieth Century Society, London, 2000.

MONOGRAPHS *(architects and clients)*

Archer, Lucy, *Raymond Erith, Architect*, Cygnet Press, Burford, 1985.

Aslet, Clive, *Quinlan Terry: The Revival of Architecture*, Viking, London, 1986.

Brown, Jane, *A Garden and Three Houses* [Peter Aldington], Garden Art Press, Woodbridge, 1999.

Edwards, Brian, *Basil Spence*, The Rutland Press, Edinburgh, 1995.

Harwood, Elain and Powers, Alan, *Tayler and Green, Architects, 1938–1973: The Spirit of Place in Modern Housing*, The Prince of Wales's Institute of Architecture, London, 1998.

Haslam, Richard, *Clough Williams-Ellis*, Academy Editions, London, 1996.

Hussey, Christopher, *The Life of Sir Edwin Lutyens*, Country Life Books, London, 1950.

Powell, Kenneth, *Edward Cullinan, Architect*, Academy Editions, London, 1995.

—, *Richard Rogers. Team 4, Richard & Su Rogers, Piano & Rogers, Richard Rogers Partnership. Complete Works*, vol. 1, Phaidon, London, 1999.

Powers, Alan, *Oliver Hill: Architect and Lover of Life*, Mouton Publications, London, 1989.

—, *John Campbell: Rediscovery of an Arts and Crafts Architect*, The Prince of Wales's Institute of Architecture, London, 1997.

—, *Francis Pollen, Architect*, Robert Dugdale, Oxford, 1999.

— (with Simon Houfe and John Wilton Ely), *Sir Albert Richardson, 1880–1964*, Heinz Gallery, London, 1999.

—, *Serge Chermayeff, Designer, Architect, Teacher*, RIBA Publications, London, 2001.

Robinson, John Martin and Neave, David, *Francis Johnson, Architect, a Classical Statement*, Oblong Creative, Otley, 2001.

Sharp, Dennis, *Connell, Ward and Lucas*, Book Art, London, 1995.

Stamp, Gavin, *Edwin Lutyens Country Houses: From the Archives of Country Life*, Aurum Press, London, 2001.

Stansky, Peter, *Sassoon: The Worlds of Philip and Sibyl*, Yale University Press, London, 2003.

Terry, Quinlan, *Quinlan Terry, Selected Works*, Academy Editions, London, 1993.

Tilden, Philip, *True Remembrances: The Memoirs of an Architect*, Country Life Books, London, 1954.

Williams-Ellis, Clough, *Architect Errant*, Constable, London, 1971.

GUIDEBOOKS FOR HOUSES OPEN TO THE PUBLIC

Dartington Hall Trust, *High Cross House*.

English Heritage, *Eltham Palace*.

The National Trust, *2 Willow Road*.

The National Trust, *Coleton Fishacre*.

The National Trust, *The Homewood*.